Dawn Eden Goldstein

Sunday Will Never Be the Same

Catholic Answers Press

Published by Catholic Answers, Inc.
2020 Gillespie Way
El Cajon, California 92020
1-888-291-8000 orders
619-387-0042 fax
catholic.com

Printed in the United States of America

Cover design by Steve Stanley
Interior design by Russell Graphic Design

978-1-68357-119-3
978-1-68357-120-9 Kindle
978-1-68357-121-6 ePub

To Ken Easton and Michelle Thompson,
with gratitude in the Lord

Contents

Acknowledgments

Thanks are due first to my family, especially my mother, father, sister, brother, stepmother, and stepfather (who is now, in a happy postscript to the events of this book, also my godson). I love you all dearly and could not have written this book without your support, patience, understanding, and love.

For many years, people have asked me to write about my faith journey. However, it wasn't until my friend Kevin Turley urged me to do so that I realized I was capable of undertaking a memoir. Kevin has a charism for inspiration; my gratitude goes out to him and his wife, Kitty.

Thanks too, very much, to my publishers and agents past and present, especially Christopher Check, Todd Aglialoro, Darin DeLozier, Cy Kellett, and everyone at Catholic Answers; Kristi McDonald, Tom Grady, and all at Ave Maria Press; Wes Yoder and all at the Ambassador Literary Agency; Janet Rosen, and Sheree Bykofsky.

Many thanks to the leadership of Holy Apostles College and Seminary and my previous employer, St. Mary's College, Oscott, for your patience and generosity as I worked on this memoir.

I am also deeply grateful to all my friends and to all who have encouraged me, especially William Doino, Jr.; Mike Aquilina; Fr. Timothy Bellamah, O.P.; Fr. Phil Bloom; Irwin Chusid; Fr. John Corbett, O.P.; Ken Easton; Robert Fastiggi; Fr. Angelo Mary Geiger, O.F.M. Conv.; Fr. Michael Gilmary, M.M.A.; Fr. Gregory Gresko, O.S.B.; Fr. Brendan Guilfoil; Fr. William Gurnee; Kevin Knight; Fr. John Baptist Ku, O.P.; Matthew and Joy Levering; Br. John Luth, M.I.C.; Michael Mazzarella; Alexandra Molotkow; Lori Stibitz; Fr. Paul Mankowski, S.J.; Fr. Nick Parker; Fr.

Sean Raftis; Kathy Schmugge; Steve Stanley; Luba Timchinna; Fr. Joseph Tito; and Fr. Augustine Wetta, O.S.B.

In memoriam: Peter Birrell; Fr. Francis Canavan, S.J.; Fr. John Edwards, S.J.; Jeff Hendrix; Faith Abbott McFadden; Stephanie Nooney; Archbishop Pietro Sambi; my grandparents; Aunt Alma.

Finally, I would like to apologize to anyone I have hurt who may be reading this. All whom I have hurt and all who have hurt me are always in my prayers.

Don't Pass
Me By

EMILY: Do any human beings ever realize life
while they live it—every, every minute?
STAGE MANAGER: No. Saints and poets
maybe—they do some.

—Thornton Wilder, *Our Town*

I don't recommend living in a fantasy world, but there were times during my college years when a good daydream was the only thing preventing me from jumping off the roof. Well, that and the thought that my last breath would be taken atop a pile of discarded beer cans, cigarette stubs, and condoms in the narrow crevice separating my New York University dormitory from the building next door.

The fantasy I have in mind began with me walking along University Place, just down the block from where I lived, and finding myself face-to-face with a strange yet familiar figure: my older self.

Mature Dawn had mysteriously transported back from fifteen or twenty years in the future. Unlike my college-age self, she was thin and she looked natural, not overly made up. (If I were grading myself on prophecy, I would give myself fifty percent.) I imagined her walking with me as a wise, motherly best friend. She told me that there were good things ahead for me, so I needed to buck up and get on with the business of living.

I mention this because in writing this book, as I faced the challenge of tracing the threads of grace connecting my spiritual journey from Judaism to agnosticism, Protestantism, and finally to Catholicism, I found myself once more fantasizing about the Dawn of the future.

This time, I envisioned myself in a care facility, having lost some of my memory through age-related illness or a debilitating accident. With that mental picture in place, a question took possession of my imagination: If some kind visitor were to attempt to remind me of who I was and what my life had been like, what could he say that would restore my self-understanding?

As I contemplated this scenario, with lots of environmental details that I won't bore you with (even my older self is thinner than I am), it seemed to me that the best way to tell my story would be not to "tell" it at all—at least, not in the usual manner of "and then I did this," etc. Rather, I needed to *show* it. I needed to show how God worked through my experiences—even through my ignorance, my mistakes, and my sins—to draw me into a closer relationship with him. And the best way to do that would be to capture my feelings and reactions as they happened, in the present tense.

Granted, the unfiltered, "you are there" approach has its drawbacks. Because the focus is upon a particular slice of time in my spiritual history, the impressions that come through of other people capture only how they appeared to me at that particular moment. At various points, a slice of time reveals that I made a negative judgment upon an individual—sometimes even a member of my family. But there are layers above and below the particular stratum that is brought to light here and now. The story continues.

The approach also means there are inevitably going to be some loose ends. I have worked to ensure that, apart from the fact that my own happy ending is still in progress—and will be as long as I am on this side of heaven—all the major plot threads in this book are resolved. If some minor threads stick out, so be it. I would rather take that risk than knit my story together so tightly that there is no room for the Holy Spirit to act upon readers' minds and hearts. I pray that the same Spirit will use this book as an instrument to reach you with the divine love that has given me healing and hope.

1 God Only Knows

Saturday, March 9, 1974, afternoon. I am five and a half years old.

Wish I didn't have to wear my sandals. But I have to put them on because I'm going out to the back yard and there might be sticker burs.

I push open the sliding glass doors in our living room. It takes two hands. A few quick steps over our back patio and I am walking on the grass.

When we lived in New York, we had birch trees in our back yard. We have trees here too, but we also have something more. We have the water.

If I stand in our yard like I am now, with my back to the house, I see green, pink, gray, and more gray.

The green is the grass. The pink is the granite rocks that start where the grass stops. The gray is the water of Galveston Bay that laps up against the rocks. It's not really gray. It just looks gray because that's how the sky is today.

Across the bay is Seawolf Park, where they have a real submarine. I can just about see the submarine's outlines. If it was sunny, I would be able to read the numbers on its side.

But I don't care about the clouds, not really. It just feels good to be outside. There is nothing to do indoors but read or watch TV. My sister Jennifer is at her friend's. Daddy is out of town. Mommy is in bed.

Mommy is in bed almost all the time lately. She will say, "I'm going into my own world now," which means not to bother her.

I don't know why she sleeps so much. I think it has to do with the separation. Mommy and Daddy are not going to be married anymore.

I can't tell yet what's going to be different. I will miss Daddy, but I miss him already because he is gone so much for his work. And when he is here, he and Mommy argue. Maybe no more marriage means no more arguing.

Still, if I think about it, it will make me sad. So I won't think about it. I will look for four-leaf clovers and sing the song about them I learned in school.

There is a big patch of clover a few steps away from me. I start to walk over. Then I catch myself. I stop walking—just for a moment—and stand there. The reason I stop is that I want to imagine: what would my life be like if I didn't stop? If I kept walking?

Grown-ups say I daydream. I do. I just can't get over how everything I do, every move I make, changes my life.

Maybe it doesn't make a big difference if I stop before walking over to the clover. But what if it does?

Another thing I like to do is to look out of windows at people walking by and imagine what it must like to be them. I do that a lot when I'm in a car or on a bus.

To me, the people walking by are just strangers. They have nothing to do with my life. But to them, *I* am a stranger, just some kid in a car—if they even notice me at all. They keep going their way. Where are they going, and why are they going there?

Everything they do matters to them more than it ever could matter to me. Because I am not them. Just thinking about it amazes me.

On Sundays, me and Jennifer go to Sunday school. When I told Grandpa Buddy about it over the phone, he called it Hebrew school. But we are Reform Jewish and we call it Sunday school.

In my class, we learned about Adam and Eve, and we learned about Noah. God created Adam and Eve. But after a while, people forgot that God made them, and they became bad—everyone except Noah. So God made a flood to wash away the bad people.

I don't understand how people could have forgotten God made them. It's not like we could make ourselves. I mean, I know daddies and mommies make babies. But someone had to make the first daddy and mommy.

I think about things like that a lot. About life and what it means. That's why I like the Peanuts comic strip, because it talks about things like that. There is the one where Lucy asks Charlie Brown, "Why are we here on earth?" And he says, "To make others happy." Then Lucy says, "What are the others here for?"

I look up from the clover and try to make out where the sun is hiding behind the clouds.

Grown-ups tell me God is not something that I could draw. Mommy likes to say he is not an old man in the sky. God is spirit. And they tell me God is infinite.

Space is infinite too. I know what they mean when they say space is infinite. It goes on and on and never ends.

But I don't know for sure what they mean when they say God is infinite.

When I try to imagine it, I think about how God made the world. Everything in the world is because God is.

God is real. This world I experience is real. But God was before everything else. Before the big leafy tree in the back yard, before the grass, before the clover, before the rocks, before the water, before me. So God must somehow be more real than everything else. Because everything else is just a thought in his mind.

Sometimes I wonder, if I thought hard enough, if I could somehow find my way behind that thought—God's thought of everything. If I could find my way behind the thought back to the one who is thinking—all the way back to God.

I am thinking about those things today. The gray bay in front of me has lots of tiny ripples. Why are we here on earth? What is the meaning of life?

Suddenly a thought flashes in my head and now it is the only thing I can think about. Love. *Love!* The answer to everything is love!

I feel excited! This is *good news*! I have to tell Mommy. Everyone has to stop what they are doing and love one another. If everyone just loved one another, there would be no fighting, no wars . . .

No, I will not tell Mommy. I will not tell her, because I don't want to sound stupid. That thought, that feeling—it all went by so quick. Like lightning at night that takes away the dark with a flash. For a flash, I understood everything. It was all so clear. Like I was touching God.

But now I look out again, I see the green, the pink, the gray and more gray, and that thought, that feeling—it's all slipping away, and I can't make it come back, even though I try and try . . .

Friday, August 2, 1974, evening. Mommy, my sister, and me are in temple for the Shabbat service. A lot of sitting down and standing up. There is a prayer book, but I am having trouble following it. I will be on one page and it will say, "On Rosh Hodesh, go to page 172," or something like that, and everyone else will know when to flip to another page and when to stay on the same one, but I can't figure it out.

I find something like wax stuck to my green velvet seat, so I try to peel it off. What I really want to do right now is read. But there is nothing to read here except the prayer book and the book of Torah readings.

So I whisper, "Mommy, can I go to the library?" Our temple has its own library. There's not much there for kids to read. But it's quiet and I can be in my own world.

Mommy nods. She knows I can find the library by myself.

The temple is like our second home. It has a school, Temple Academy, where I went to pre-K and kindergarten. Soon I will go back there for first grade.

In the library now. I found an old book I want to read, *The Adventures of K'Ton Ton*, and am sitting on a folding chair. Mommy would smile if she saw me, because I am sitting the way I always sit: Indian style. Grown-ups think it's hard to sit like this, but it's my favorite. It feels better than letting my legs dangle.

I am wearing a green jumper dress with a white blouse underneath, short white socks, and brown leather shoes. Oh, yes, and underwear. It feels nice to wear socks instead of tights. I hate tights. They're itchy.

"Well, hullo, l'il lady. What you doin' in here?"

I look up to see Al standing in the doorway. Al's real name is Alfonse but people call him Al. He is the janitor and I usually only see him in the hall with his mop and bucket.

Al is old and black. We have a black maid at home named Waldine who does not know how to read. I can't believe that a grown-up isn't able to read. I am five going on six and I have been reading for two whole years. But Mommy told me Waldine never learned to read because she is poor. Mommy says so many black people are poor because white people are—I think she said prejudiced. Prejudice means thinking bad things about people because of the color of their skin.

Mommy says there is a lot of prejudice here in Texas. There wasn't so much when we lived in New York. So we should be nice to black people, because lots of people are mean to them.

I don't really like Al. I don't know why, I just don't. But I don't want to be prejudiced. If I am nice to him, it will make Mommy happy.

"Just reading. My mommy said I could come in here to read."

Al just stands and stares for a moment. Then he walks up and leans over me. "What's a l'il girl like you readin'?"

I close the book's cover to show him. My thumb saves my place.

"That's some book, all right."

He is quiet now, like he is thinking. Then he speaks again.

"I'se nothin' to do. You play a game with me?"

"A game?"

Why would a grown-up want to take me away from reading? Something is wrong but I don't know what it is.

"I show you. Come on."

Al grasps my arm and takes me to the door. Then he says, "Wait." He looks out the doorway. Then he takes me down the empty hall, past the restrooms, to the telephone booth.

Friday, August 30, 1974, afternoon. School is done for the day. I am playing with my friend Linda in a corner of our first-grade classroom. We are sitting facing each other in a wooden rocker toy shaped like a little ship. It reminds me of a song I heard on the radio. I start singing, "Rock the boat! Rock the boat!"

Mommy shows up at the door. She is here to pick me up. Her face has that look it gets when she is coming down with a migraine.

I want to ask Mommy what the rabbi said, but I don't want anyone else to know. It will have to wait until we get in the car.

We walk down the hall, past the restrooms, past the phone booth. Al's mop and bucket are there, but no sign of Al. Good.

Last week I told Mommy about Al's game. I was scared to tell her. Al told me to keep it a secret. And I wanted to keep it a secret because it felt so wrong and I didn't want to get in trouble. But when I thought about it—especially after the second time Al found me and took me down the hall—I couldn't keep a secret from Mommy. We never have secrets. And I was scared too that Al would want to take me down the hall again. So I told.

As soon as I told Mommy, I wished I hadn't. She got really mad. Mad at Al. Mad at me. I can still hear her words in my head: *You let him do that to you!*

Mommy couldn't understand why I went back to the library after what Al did to me the first time. I think she thinks I must have wanted him to find me again. I didn't. But there was no way I could explain it to her.

After Mommy thought about it a while, she was not really mad at me. She told me I let Al do what he did because I missed Daddy.

I told Mommy that wasn't true. I think about it now as we walk out to the car and it still isn't true. I do miss Daddy, but it's not like I never get to see him. Me and my sister see him every Saturday. And Daddy would never play a game like Al's. But Mommy thinks I let Al do bad things because I wanted "affection." So it is really all my fault, but she is not mad at me.

But Mommy is mad at Al. That is why she decided to see the rabbi today and tell him Al should be fired. I want him fired too so I will never have to see him again.

Now Mommy and me are in the car. When she turns the key, the radio comes on: "I shot the sheriff . . ."

Mommy hits a button. Now the only sounds are the motor and the air conditioning.

Her face tells me her meeting with the rabbi went bad. I wait for her to speak.

"I told him what happened. He was very surprised, because Al is seventy-three years old and is a deacon in his church. Also, Al has been working at B'nai Israel for over twenty years.

"So he called Al into his office, told him what I said, and asked if it was true.

"Al said, 'That sweet little girl? No sir! I didn't do nothin' to that little girl.'"

I gasp. "You mean he lied!" I can't believe he would lie. Lying is a sin!

Mommy keeps talking. She is not happy. The rabbi told her that, because Al denied my "story," he couldn't fire Al.

That means the rabbi thinks I am a liar. And I will still have to see Al at school.

Mommy knows what I am thinking. "You don't have to worry. Al won't bother you anymore. I warned him never to go near you again."

I know Mommy can't go against the rabbi. Daddy might do that if he knew. But Mommy hasn't told Daddy what happened. And if she doesn't tell him, I can't either. What if he blamed me too? Or what if he blamed Mommy? Then they would start arguing again. So I can't say anything.

Saturday, April 24, 1976, evening. I am bored. All around me are grown-ups in grown-up conversations. The only kids I know here are Jennifer's friends, but they are all talking and laughing with her. Even Grandma Mimi and Grandma Jessie are paying more attention to grown-ups and to my sister than they are to me.

It would be more interesting if this was *my* party. But everyone is here at the Hotel Galvez to celebrate Jennifer's bat mitzvah.

Some of the grown-ups stop to tell me that in five years they'll come back for my bat mitzvah. They think that will make me happy. It doesn't. Five years feels like a lifetime. It really is, too. It's more than half my life.

I walk across the room to get another cup of fruit punch. On my right is a table covered with envelopes and gift boxes in different sizes. I know my sister deserves them. At the ceremony, she chanted beautifully in Hebrew. She also led the singing and gave a good sermon. But I have had all I can take of this bat-mitzvah stuff. All I can think about now is going home, looking at my Peanuts books and Archie comics, and going to bed.

A man my dad's age, sitting at a table, sees me as I try to walk past him. He stands up and reaches out to catch my attention. "Excuse me, Dawn?" He seems shy for a grown-up.

I have never seen this man before. He is wearing a tan suit and holding a white paper shopping bag, the kind with handles. Standing by him is a girl in a short-sleeved ruffled dress who looks about four. She has brown hair with bangs peeking out below her hairband. Her left hand is at her mouth; she is sucking on her fingertips.

The man tries to speak to me. I have a hard time hearing him over all the music and conversation. He says something about knowing my sister from her school. That probably means he's Christian. Temple Academy only goes up to the third grade, so Jennifer goes to Trinity Episcopal School.

"We brought a gift for your sister, but we wanted to give something to you too."

The man hands the bag to his daughter to give to me. She has to take her hand out of her mouth to hold it. It is heavy for a little girl. But she is even more shy than her dad; she hands me the bag without saying anything. She doesn't even smile. So "we brought a gift" must really just mean her father brought it.

I say thank you and put my hand inside the bag, pulling out a book. It is unwrapped but new: *Children's Stories of the Bible from the Old and New Testaments.* On the cover are a few pictures of Bible scenes; the biggest one has Jesus seated at a long table. I know it is Jesus because it looks like a picture I saw in the church basement where I go for Girl Scout meetings.

"A book! I love books. Thank you."

I am trying my hardest to be nice. It really is kind of the man to remember me on a day when my sister is the one who is supposed to get presents. But if Mommy heard me, she would know I am being fake. I force one last smile at the man and start again toward the punch bowls.

I like the Bible, but this is a *Christian* book. It amazes me that a man would give the sister of the bat-mitzvah girl a Christian book. How stupid can a person be? Doesn't he know Jews don't read the New Testament?

It's not like I have anything against Jesus. Mommy and Daddy both say he was a teacher and a good man. Also, at

Mommy's house, we have the original-cast albums of *God-spell* and *Jesus Christ Superstar*, so I know the Jesus story. But we are Jews and we don't believe Jesus was God. If he was God, things would be a lot different than they are. His coming would have changed everything.

I can't stop thinking about how stupid that man is. Don't Christians know anything about Jews?

Sunday, April 25, 1976, 10:03 p.m. I am in my bedroom in the apartment where I live with Mommy and my sister. I have school tomorrow and I should be going to bed. But I am not sleepy yet, so I look at *Children's Stories from the Old and New Testaments*. It is a good book to look at when I am not sleepy, because it is the longest book I own—two hundred and fifty-four pages.

Actually, the book is a lot better than I expected. I thought it would talk down to me like the Christian children's books I see in doctor's offices. But in fact its stories read more like the way they are told the Bible itself, only the words are simpler, without the thee's and thou's. And there's nothing in it about Jews going to hell or any of that crazy stuff.

Interesting to see how the stories about Jesus come after the stories about Old Testament prophets. It's as if the Old and New Testaments were two halves of one book. I like the things Jesus says. But of course he can't be God, because then all his miracles would be true, and if all his miracles were true, he would have converted the whole world.

Wednesday, October 20, 1976, 10:25 p.m. Sitting in bed with my knees up and the book of Bible stories open in my lap. It's a school night and I should be asleep. But there is no one around to notice I'm still up.

Well, that's not exactly true. Jennifer is home but she is in her room and she gets mad if I want to come in. She likes to read and she says I bother her. Mommy is out with her boyfriend Michael.

I'm scared. It shouldn't scare me to be home when Mommy is out. Lots of times I am here alone before Jennifer comes home from school and Mommy comes home from work. When I started third grade last month, Mommy gave me a key to let myself in. I wear it to school on a string around my neck.

But sometimes, when I'm home alone, bad men come to our door.

Our apartment is on the second floor. It has an outdoor entrance on a balcony next to other apartments and anyone can walk up. When the bad men come, I can see them through the peephole if I stand on tiptoe. Sometimes they come in groups of two or three, and they smoke cigarettes. They don't always ring the bell. Sometimes they just stand there, waiting.

Once when a bad man stood outside our front door, I shouted at him, trying to sound grown-up: "What do you want?"

"You," he said. Then he laughed and walked away.

I am also scared of fires. At school last week a fireman came in to teach us about fire prevention. He showed us slides of kids at the Shriners Burns Institute so we could see what happens to kids who play with fire.

The pictures were horrible. They showed kids' faces all shriveled and blackened. I don't know why I have to look at those things when I never wanted to play with fire anyway.

What if there was a fire and everyone died but me? Or what if there was a fire at Daddy's house and he and my stepmother died?

Things like that are too awful to imagine. I can't get by from day to day if I worry about such things. I just can't.

Maybe I can make a deal with God.

Dear God, I will read something from this book of Bible stories every night. And you will protect me.

I am not going to worry now.

Sunday, October 1, 1978, 8:25 p.m. My sister is out with her friends, but Mom and her new boyfriend Henry are watching the ABC Sunday Night Movie with me. They are sitting together on the couch by our front window. I am in a chair on the other side of the coffee table. We are all looking at the movie on our little black-and-white TV.

Soon we will have a color TV. Henry has an extra one he is going to give us. He does not need it now that he has moved into an apartment. Before that, he lived with his wife, but they just broke up. They had a baby that is one month old.

I liked Mom's last real boyfriend, Michael. Sometimes he could be a pain—he was bossy—but he respected me and my sister, and he tried to act dignified around us.

Even though Mom and Michael broke up, she keeps the picture he gave her on the wall by her bed. It comes from Athens and shows an angel called Michael holding a sword and something that looks like a globe. Mom calls it the Ark Angel.

Henry doesn't give Mom art. He is tall like Michael and has a beard like him. But other than that, the two of them are as different as can be.

For one thing, Henry does not watch his mouth. Every other word he says is the s-word or worse. Once when we were in the car, I complained about his using the s-word and Mom tried to stand up for me. But when Henry got angry and said there was nothing wrong with his language, she backed down.

Sometimes Henry does something else Michael never did. He walks around without clothes on. I am used to Mom doing that, especially when she has a migraine and her clothes make her feel too sweaty. But now she and Henry both do it.

They never do it when Jennifer is home, though. Mom told me that is because my sister is modest. Modest means being embarrassed at things you shouldn't be embarrassed about.

To tell the truth, I am jealous of my sister not having to look at them. I would like to be modest too. But I like it when Mom says I am easier to get along with than Jennifer, because my sister is better than me in everything except spelling. So I try not to complain and to go along with Mom in everything. It makes me feel special when she tells me I am her best friend.

The ABC movie tonight is a made-for-TV drama. I wanted to watch the sitcoms on CBS but was outvoted. Right now, there is a close-up of a man and a woman kissing. It looks so weird, like they're eating each other. It doesn't look like love. And it goes on and on.

I sigh. "What are they *doing* when their mouths are together like that?"

Henry turns his eyes away from the TV screen. "What?"

"I mean, I know they're kissing. But what are they doing with their mouths when they kiss like that?"

Henry begins to say something to me, but then he stops and turns to my mother. Like he wants to ask if it's okay for him to do something.

Friday, September 11, 1981, 4:55 p.m. Our kitchen clock says five p.m., but Mom keeps it five minutes fast, so it's really just five to five. Mom should be home any minute.

I'm ready. As soon as I came home from school, I changed into the dress and matching wedge sandals that Grandma Jessie bought me a couple of weeks ago at the Short Hills Mall.

The sandals are not really fancy enough for a bat-mitzvah girl. They are also too summery for September in New Jersey—in fact, that's probably why they were on sale. But they were the only ones I could find that matched the blue in my dress. I really love the dress. It is long and billowy, made of soft Indian cotton.

I know I should be practicing my Torah portion, which I will be chanting in Hebrew. For months, I have been learning it from a cassette made for me by my temple's cantor. But I just can't concentrate right now. The only thing I am capable of doing at the moment is walking outside to watch for Mom.

Our house is on the edge of South Orange's Grove Park, a green rectangle a few blocks long. From our little wedge of lawn, I can see children laughing as they take turns going down the playground slide.

Yellow sunrays shine through the trees at an early-evening angle. The light, the breeze, a certain kind of leafy smell in the air—all these things combine to hit me with a feeling of wistful sadness.

I recognize the feeling. It usually hits me around the time of my birthday, which was last week. Turning another year older right at the start of the school year, just when the summer wind starts to take on a cool edge—it makes me think about time passing, and then this feeling comes out of nowhere. There is one day a year when I really feel it. This must be the day.

Today I have another reason to think about the passage of time. My bat mitzvah—just two and a half hours away—marks the start of my life as a Jewish woman. In the eyes of

the law, I may be five years from adulthood, but in the eyes
of Jewish law, I am an adult from the moment I go up for my
aliyah, when I read from the Torah.

My mind goes back to this time last year. Mom and I
had just arrived in New Jersey from Galveston and were
staying with Grandma Jessie and Grandpa Buddy until she
could find a job. With my sister going to college in Washington, D.C., where Dad lives with my stepmother Linda,
and nearly all our other relatives living in the Northeast, it
didn't make sense to stay in Texas.

Since I had just turned twelve, one of the first things on
Mom's agenda upon moving up north was to get us a family membership at a temple so I could prepare for my bat
mitzvah. She found a Reform temple that put me on their
calendar. So far, so good. But we ran up against resistance
when Mom told the rabbi I wanted to do like my sister did
and lead practically the entire ceremony.

The problem is, with there being so many more Jewish kids here than there were in Galveston, Temple Israel
does its bat- and bar mitzvahs like an assembly line. Each
kid gets a cassette tape from the cantor with the melodies
they have to know to chant their *aliyah* along with their
parasha and *haftarah*—the weekly Torah portion and the
reading from the prophets—and that's the extent of their
participation. Everything else in the service is decided
by the rabbi and cantor. If a kid wants to deliver a *d'var
Torah*, saying a few words about the readings, the rabbi
assigns a topic rather than giving the kid the chance to
pick out what he or she thinks is most important from the
scripture passages.

So Mom had to persuade Rabbi Weiner and Cantor Levitt to let me pick out the service's music and to write my
own *d'var Torah*. It took some doing, but they finally agreed,

though the cantor raised a fuss when I asked if I could lead most of the songs myself.

Normally, going to Shabbat at Temple Israel is almost like going to an opera recital. Cantor Levitt is a classically trained composer whose work is performed in New York. When he leads the music, he uses fancy melodies that he wrote. They're designed so he gets all the verses. The rest of us can try to sing along to the chorus, but even that's hard because he writes for his own voice, a high tenor.

Cantor Levitt refused to give up singing key hymns such as "Lecha Dodi," the song that welcomes the Sabbath as though it were a bride. So I asked that he at least use the melodies everyone knows, instead of his own. He agreed, but only very reluctantly.

Another problem came up as I started to write my *d'var Torah*. It just so happened that the *parasha* for the week of my bat mitzvah was the toughest Torah portion of the whole year—full of weird little laws. So Mom went to the rabbi again and got him to agree to meet with me to answer my questions.

Unfortunately, the meeting did not go well.

I arrived armed with a list of the most challenging passages in my *parasha*. Some of them were embarrassing to even mention, like Deuteronomy 23:2, though the old translation made it sound even odder than it was: "He that is crushed or maimed in his privy parts shall not enter into the assembly of the Lord." Wasn't that unfair to men who were wounded through no fault of their own?

Other passages were just confusing, like Deuteronomy 21:23, where it says that "he that is hanged is a reproach unto God." How could a hanged man be a "reproach unto God" if he had committed an offense that the Torah said was worthy of death? And how did any of this relate to the *haftarah*—a passage from Isaiah 54 about a barren woman singing?

But once I sat down with Rabbi Weiner, I was only able to run down a couple of passages off my list before he interrupted me. He told me that scholars spent their entire lives answering such questions. There was no way such verses could be explained to someone who has not studied Torah and Talmud. Therefore I should forget about writing my *d'var Torah* about my *parasha*. "Just do it on your *haftarah*," he said with a dismissive throw of his hand.

I came out of the meeting angry and hurt. The rabbi treated me like I was a stupid child instead of a sincere student seeking to better understand the faith of her ancestors. But as I think about it now, watching the children playing in the early-evening sunlight, I realize it doesn't matter what he thinks of me. All that matters is the moment I stand on the *bimah* at the center of the sanctuary and show the congregation that I have grown from a girl to a woman.

The sunlight's angle changes once more and that fall feeling comes again—a sense of longing. Justin Hayward's song "Forever Autumn" runs through my mind. "My life will be forever autumn, 'cause you're not here . . . 'cause you're not here . . ."

Why do I feel sad? Who is not here?

I want a boyfriend, someone to love me. And I want God to love me too.

Usually I do not think of those two things at the same time. Maybe it has something to do with wanting to be a woman. I want to be a woman with a man and I want to be a woman before God.

The thought makes me sad but also hopeful. Maybe God has plans for me. Maybe he wants to make me happy, to fulfill my dreams.

The breeze seems to pass right through me. Inside me it feels like a wave of thankfulness, tinged with hope. *Thank you, God. Thank you for bringing me to this day I have awaited for so long. I'm excited to see what you have in store for me.*

Two and a half hours later. The service is about to begin. As I walk up to take my place in the sanctuary, Cantor Levitt approaches me.

"There's not enough for me to do," he says. "We're going to do 'Lecha Dodi' my way."

And just like that he walks off to take his place by the organist.

All eyes are on me now. There is nothing I can do. I can't even let my expression show how stunned I am. All those feelings I felt after that meeting with Rabbi Weiner come back. I'm hurt, angry, furious.

How could the cantor change the music at the last minute just to get his moment in the spotlight? What kind of person does that?

About two hours later. At the *oneg*, the reception after the ceremony, I am taking in compliments and congratulations from all sides and trying to smile despite the tension of having Mom in the same room as Dad and Linda. Fortunately, right now they have something pleasant they can talk about together. They are all very proud of me and are telling each other how well I did.

I am chatting with a friend from school when Mom interrupts to introduce me to a neatly dressed older woman who has short hair and gold earrings. The woman tells me she has been coming to Temple Israel for thirty years and has never seen such a beautiful service.

It is very nice of the woman to say that. I gently shake her hand and thank her. But inside, I have no desire to have anything more to do with Temple Israel—or any temple.

2 Spirit in the Sky

Wednesday, March 13, 1985, 2:39 p.m. "Now that I've seen Livingston College," I say to Mom, "I don't think I'd want to go there. If I went to any college here, it would be Rutgers College."

It was good of Mom to take the day off work so we could tour the schools on the New Brunswick campus of Rutgers University. If I'm not admitted into the music-business program at New York University, the state university of New Jersey is my second choice.

We are walking through the student center now. It is lined with convention-style tables where student groups promote their activities.

A young woman off to our right calls out, "Free Bibles!"

Mom and I turn to look at the table where the woman is trying to grab our attention. Hanging along its edge is a banner for Campus Crusade for Christ.

Atop the table are several neat small stacks of a paperback that I would not have recognized as a Bible. It has the words "Good News" on its cover, but instead of a cross or an image of Jesus, it has faces of men and women of different races and ages.

Mom picks a book off one of the stacks, holding it quizzically as she would if she were trying to assess the ripeness of a tomato.

"What do you think," she asks me. "Should I take one? It's free."

Should she? It's not like there's any shortage of spiritual reading material at our apartment. Our living room is lined with religious and New Age books. When I was bored as a child, I would page through them, trying to keep track of the innumerable gods and goddesses in the *Bhagavad-Gita* or wondering how the Mormons could bear having a prophet named Moroni.

Do we need a New Testament? No. I know for a fact that we have a King James somewhere. But maybe it would be worthwhile for Mom to read the Good News Bible, if only to stop her seeking.

For years, she has carted me along with her to sit at the feet of different yogis, self-help gurus, and others claiming higher wisdom. I'm willing to go because I like being her best friend, even though it can be demanding. It helps make up for Dad's distance.

Dad met and married Linda soon after the divorce. Then, when I was nine, they moved thousands of miles away. Now they have a child of their own, my brother Adam, and I feel like yesterday's news. Once or twice a month Dad calls to ask how I am doing in school, but he doesn't seem interested in my day-to-day life. He and Linda let me visit them only a week or two out of the year.

So I'm all right with Mom bringing me to her kundalini yoga classes and self-help conferences and Whole Life Expos. But I am starting to suspect that all the New Age stuff is pointless, because each teacher contradicts the last.

Mom's latest spiritual teacher is Hilda, a woman in her late seventies who wears a sari. Hilda was a modern dancer until she found enlightenment in India. Every Thursday night, hundreds of people pack the basement of the mammoth Episcopalian Cathedral of St. John the Divine on Manhattan's Upper West Side to hear her lecture. Mom is one of them; others include rich and famous people like record-label executive Danny Goldberg. It's said that Goldberg once arrived for Hilda's lecture in a limousine with Diana Ross on his arm.

Hilda can seem like a sweet and grandmotherly lady, but some of her teachings are disturbing. One week, she spoke matter-of-factly that we should prepare for a great famine— though she added we had nothing to worry about because the aliens would come and save us.

During the ride home that night, I asked Mom if she really believed Hilda's predictions. She assured me she tuned them out. What she liked were Hilda's teachings on how to be a better and more loving person. The following Thursday, she was back among the huddled masses in St. John the Divine's basement, still hearkening to Hilda's spacey sermons in hope of extracting some wisdom for everyday life.

So, what do I say to Mom as she stands before me in the student center at Rutgers with a New Testament in her hand? What I really want to say to her is, please, Mom, find a spirituality that's not flaky.

So, then, should she read the Bible? I look Mom in the eyes and raise my eyebrows the way I do when I am trying to sound authoritative. "Yes, Mom, you should. I read it in eighth grade and it was good."

"Really? In eighth grade?"

I thought she knew. Normally I tell her everything. But I had a lot going on in eighth grade, so maybe I didn't mention it.

"Yes. Mr. Snyder had us read the Gospels because he said they were important for understanding Western civilization."

I suspect Owen M. Snyder was the only social-studies teacher in America who could get away with bringing public-school kids, most of us Jewish, into a circle to discuss the Gospels. He was able to do it because, to us and our parents, he enjoyed godlike status—an extraordinary educator. Instead of talking down to us like other teachers, he treated us like equals, challenging us to understand college-level material. We who were fortunate enough to be admitted into his class considered ourselves his intellectual protégés, a breed apart from our peers.

Mr. Snyder's Bible lessons weren't like Sunday school. He simply showed us what the Gospels said about who Jesus was and what he said and did. That way, we would know the basic outlines of Christian belief.

A lot of what he taught us about the Gospels was technical, meant to show us how to read them. When we noticed differences between two or three Gospels' accounts of the same event, Mr. Snyder explained that they were written by eyewitnesses, and different eyewitnesses notice different things.

Mostly we discussed the moral teachings of the Sermon on the Mount. There was no test that I can recall. I found the class discussion and reading assignments interesting, but I took them in the spirit in which they were given—as information, not inspiration.

One thing I knew for sure: Jesus' teachings were more sensible and coherent than anything I heard from New Age practitioners. In fact, the spirit of his moral teachings didn't seem too far from the things I was taught as a Jewish child, to "do justly, love mercy" and "walk humbly with your God"—the words emblazoned on the wall behind the pulpit of my childhood temple. Plus, Jesus wasn't trying to make a buck and he never mentioned space aliens. Surely he was a better spiritual guide than Hilda, even if some of his followers tried to twist his teachings to serve their own ends.

My endorsement has its desired effect upon Mom. She tucks the Good News Bible under her arm, thanking the young woman behind the table, and we continue on our way.

Friday, March 15, 1985, 10:17 p.m. Mom's light is still on and her bedroom door is open a crack. I knock so I can come in to say good night. She doesn't answer, so I take that to mean she is decent and I can walk in. These days she knows I don't like to see her when she isn't dressed.

Mom is awake in bed wearing her flannel nightgown, her head propped up on pillows. She is wearing her reading glasses and has the Good News Bible propped up on her chest. But unlike the smiling faces on its cover, her face is streaked with tears.

"Listen to this," she says. "'Happy are you when people insult you and persecute you and tell all kinds of evil lies against you . . .'"

Mom is a good reader. She reads the way she feels; the words come out strong and emotional: When people *insult* you! When they *persecute* you!

I try to seem appropriately impressed, but I don't really understand what all the fuss is about.

The words are familiar; I think they're from the Sermon on the Mount. I thought they were nice when I read them in that book of Bible stories I used to have. I thought they were nice when I read them in Mr. Snyder's class. But that's all they are—nice words.

Christians run this country. Jerry Falwell and his Moral Majority helped elect the president. But I don't see them talking about how it's a blessing to be persecuted or insulted. I see them siding with the rich over the poor and the strong over the weak.

Whatever Jesus may have said, his followers have created a different world from the one he imagined. If he was God, I can't believe he would have allowed that to happen.

Mom keeps talking. She is thinking out loud about exploring Christianity. And when she thinks of Christianity, she thinks of Catholicism, because growing up she knew only Jews and Catholics. Also, it is the oldest brand of Christianity, so there's something more authentic about it. It's the original.

I'm not going to try to talk Mom out of her emotions. She's had pain in her life and has been seeking enlightenment for a long while. If Jesus' words make her feel closer to God, then I'm happy for her.

Wednesday, July 3, 1985, 1:14 p.m. I am listening to the dB's album *Repercussion*, looking at the paper shopping bags I brought home—a large one containing a bottle of grain alcohol and a smaller one containing a box of sleeping pills—and wondering how I got to this point.

Everything changed after I graduated high school two weeks ago. I can't enjoy my summer like I did last year. The feeling of dread is too strong.

Last summer was simpler. I was lonely then like I am now, but it was easier to take my mind off of it. When I wasn't taking the chemistry class I needed in order to graduate a year early, I was blowing my allowance on transit fare to Greenwich Village.

My first stop in the city was always a little shop hidden up a dingy flight of stairs on West Eighth Street: Venus Records.

Venus is more than a place where people go to buy music. It's the center of the most exciting scene I know, the scene I'm dying to be a part of—downtown New York City's garage scene.

The local garage bands take after great mid-Sixties artists like the Beatles, Byrds, and Rolling Stones, but they go one step further. Instead of trying to recreate what those bands sounded like, they try to recreate what a group of teenagers in 1966 banging around in their parents' garage would have sounded like had *they* tried to sound like those bands.

Venus fosters the scene by stocking authentic garage records from the 1960s and today. I love going there not only to buy music but also just to people-watch. There is always some man there in a Brian Jones haircut, black stovepipe jeans, and Chelsea boots thumbing through record albums. Sometimes, too, there are young women in mod outfits peering down at the record bins, their eyelids heavy with raccoon eyeliner.

Once I discovered the scene, I wanted so badly to go to nightclubs where I could see top local garage bands like the Fuzztones, Vipers, and Cheepskates. And I did catch a few shows, with Mom's permission. Sometimes if I begged her enough, she would even take me, freeing me from the pressure of having to rush out in time to catch the last train home. The excitement of being able to stay late enough for the headlining act helped make up for the embarrassment of having my mother in tow.

Clearly the only way to realize my dream of membership in the garage scene would be to live in New York City. So that became my goal. I would graduate high school at six-teen and enter New York University, which would place me in the heart of Greenwich Village. And I wouldn't be Dawn Eden Goldstein anymore. I would just be Dawn Eden, the name I had been trying to get my high-school teachers to call me since my sophomore year.

I wanted to lose my last name because I was—am—tired of people saying, "Oh, you're Jewish." My Judaism is part of me, and I'm not ashamed of it, but it doesn't define who I am. What makes me who I am now is my love of rock and roll. And one thing I can thank my parents for is that they gave me a great rock-and-roll name.

And now I'm on the verge of fulfilling my dream. I've been admitted into NYU, where I am to live in a dorm just off Washington Square Park.

Last week, with graduation behind me, I poured my en-ergies into preparing for my grand entrance onto the garage scene. I scoured thrift shops in search of paisley shirts and miniskirts, practiced my retro-style dance moves, and twice journeyed into the city to comb East Village boutiques for the perfect shade of white lipstick. It was all great fun. I felt hopeful and free.

Best of all, Ron Rimsite—that psychedelic scarecrow with a mop of reddish-brown curly hair who works behind the counter at Venus Records—asked if I would help him with his garage fanzine *99th Floor*. He needed someone to tran-scribe a cassette of an interview with John Felice of the Real Kids. I said yes even though I have no experience transcribing anything. It was exciting just to think of getting my name into a cool underground 'zine and becoming part of Venus's orbit.

But that was last week. This week, I crashed. My old in-securities, the fears I try not to think about, are back. And they're worse than before.

It started when the question arose in my mind: *What if the garage scene failed to bring me happiness? What if my life at NYU proved to be as lonely as my life in New Jersey? What then? What would be left for me?*

I can take being unhappy, because unhappiness comes and goes. What I can't take is the ongoing sense of sadness that lingers beneath the surface even when I am having fun.

It got worse when I entered my teens. And now it's led me to the point where I have a creeping fear that, deep inside, I am incapable of being truly happy.

I always thought I would be happy if I was loved the way I wanted to be loved. That's been my fantasy since child-hood—the fairy-tale idea that I will be fulfilled by the love of a man, a husband, someone who will be the one and only love of my life, and I of his.

What scares me now is the fear that, after finding and marrying my romantic ideal, I might still feel this sadness.

What if the most basic human desire I had, the only one that could heal my sadness and make life worth living, was impossible to fulfill?

In that case, it would be better not to live.

The phone rings. I don't feel like speaking to anyone, but I'd better pick up in case it's Mom calling from work.

"Hihowyadoin. It's Derek."

Sigh. "Hi, Derek."

Derek is a kind friend. We have known each other for years and I should not be as impatient with him as I am. What annoys me about him isn't really him. It's that I wish there were a man I found attractive who would like me as much as he does.

"What're you up to?" he asks.

"Do you really want to know?"

"Sure."

I take a deep breath. "All right. I went to the drugstore today and bought sleeping pills. Then I went to the liquor store and bought grain alcohol. No one carded me. My thought was that I would take the alcohol and pills together and kill myself."

"What d'you want to do a stupid thing like that for!"

I don't feel like bothering to explain myself to Derek. He wouldn't understand anyway. So I just agree that it was stupid. He stays on the line as I flush the pills and alcohol down the toilet.

Friday, March 18, 1986, 12:23 a.m. How is it that all the smoke from all the cigarettes in this low-rent nightclub finds its way to the place right where I am standing in front of the stage? The clouds waft upward until they stagnate under the glare of the stage lights that point down at odd angles from the ceiling.

As usual, I've claimed a spot as far up front as possible, so no one can block my view. That's important since I am just short of five foot three, though the heels on my black leather ankle boots add a couple of inches.

I hate cigarette smoke. It brings back unwanted memories of parties I witnessed when I was little, where adults got tipsy or high and acted like children. Those same memories lead me to avoid drugs and alcohol, even on a night like tonight when all New York City is Irish in honor of St. Patrick. But secondhand smoke is unavoidable in nightclubs, especially this West 29th Street joint that goes by the sardonic name of the Dive. So I do the only thing possible under the circumstances: tune it out.

The stale fumes surround me, burning my eyes—yet I am able to ignore them. How is this possible? The answer is that I have chosen not to let anything separate me from what

I love. What I love is live music and the whole nightclub experience—from putting on makeup and choosing my best going-out clothes, to scanning the room for a potential new crush, to dancing without inhibition, to hearing the band answer my request for a favorite song, to screaming my lungs out for an encore.

And there is still something more that I love about it all, something I can hardly put into words.

It has to do with the fact that it is night. I enter into a dark, enclosed place where the only things that can be seen clearly are the performers and the only things that can be heard are the sounds they create—sounds that are overwhelming, all-encompassing, reverberating through my body. It's like being ravished but in a good way.

Some of the musicians are ravishing too. There is a reason my favorite ones are men. But what attracts me most is not a particular kind of face or body. It is a man who creates music from his heart.

Whenever I take my place standing before a nightclub stage, I scan the band members in hope of finding such a man. If I do, I set my desires upon him for the duration of the performance.

Usually it is the singer, as most of the bands I like are led by guitar-playing songwriters. As he sings, I long to be loved by him. I want him to love me like he loves his guitar. I want him to love me like he loves the song he wrote. I want him to love me like he loves music itself. His song itself is a gift of love.

Often, if I don't know the singer personally, I find myself wondering if he gives through his song in a way that he can't in real life. Many of the Sixties artists I admire who wrote beautiful love songs went on to leave their wives. Their love is gone; only the songs remain.

I love this song. *This* one, the one the band is playing right now. I want it to enter into my every pore, to fill and suffuse every part of me, so that there will be no part of my mind, body, and spirit that does not feel loved.

I need to drink up every drop of pleasure from nights like this, because it is only the hope of them that keeps me alive.

Although I haven't attempted suicide since that day last summer when Derek interrupted my plans, there are days and weeks when I feel perpetually choked up. At bedtime I put tissues inside my pillowcase so I won't have to reach over to the night table for them as I cry myself to sleep.

In order to keep going, my mind falls into a habit I developed when I first started wanting to die, back in high school. When suicidal thoughts come up, I think about something I'm looking forward to—usually a concert by a band I long to see—and resolve to stay alive until that event is over.

It's been easier to practice that delaying tactic since I moved into my dorm last August. No longer is my love of live music held hostage to train schedules. I can go to any Manhattan rock club I want—well, any one that admits concertgoers under twenty-one, and nearly all do. With so many artists I want to see and so many more to discover, and with live music available seven nights a week, it doesn't require much patience to survive from one concert to the next.

Tonight's show at the Dive promises, in addition to a full lineup of local bands, something special in honor of St. Patrick's Day: a late-night jam session featuring the garage scene's leading lights.

Tonight? It feels like it is still "tonight"; actually, it is almost one in the morning. I have outlasted most of the seventy or so scenemakers who took in the first three bands of the night. But it is worth it to see the jam session now beginning.

Wayne from the Secret Service gets onstage to belt out a fiery take on Johnny Kidd and the Pirates' "Shakin' All Over" backed by members of the Headless Horsemen and the Fuzztones. Then Dave from the Vipers joins in on second guitar as Bobby from the Optic Nerve takes the microphone.

"Now I'm going to do my Keith Relf impression," Bobby says, donning a pair of wrap-around sunglasses. The band tears into a poundingly authentic version of the Yardbirds' arrangement of Bo Diddley's "I'm a Man." There are more personnel switches and then, with Bobby still on vocals, they do a satisfyingly crunchy take on the Rolling Stones' "(I Can't Get No) Satisfaction." Although most of these performers have never enjoyed the interest of mainstream rock magazines, to me it's like seeing one all-star supergroup after another.

It would be even better if they played something together besides bar-band tunes. I can dance to these numbers, but they don't move me in my heart and soul.

Between songs, I call out to Peter of the Headless Horsemen, who is keeping everyone together with his steady bass lines: "Remains! Play some Remains!"

Peter looks at me and smiles. He crouches down conspiratorially so I can hear his reply over the distorted chords Dave is playing as he recalibrates his fuzzbox.

"These men can't do Remains. They're in alcoholic states."

So much for that idea. And yet, even though the songs don't take me outside of myself, something else is going on—something that moves my heart in a way I did not expect.

It occurs to me that, although the performers onstage may not be known outside the garage scene, they have all performed to packed houses at one point or another. And yet here they are in the wee hours of the morning, not playing for money or adulation or even free drinks, but only for the sheer joy of playing the music they love with musicians they admire.

I turn to gaze at the remnants of the audience. Only about two dozen fans are soldiering on now. Half of them I recognize as members of bands. Many probably have to be at work in seven or eight hours. Like me, they don't want the night to end.

This show is only tonight. Only tonight is this group of people here to experience it. Only tonight are these musicians performing alongside each other. Everyone is together with one another for only a few more minutes, until the last chord reverberates into oblivion.

I choose to live for this night, for this moment, for this experience of sharing something exciting with others that has never been before and will never be again. This is what I wanted. But even as I think these thoughts, I realize helplessly that this moment, this feeling of being part of something bigger than myself that takes me out of myself, is slipping away.

Saturday, October 4, 1986, 5:43 p.m. I am wearing my best day-into-evening outfit. On top: a bright magenta cotton turtleneck beneath my most favorite item of clothing, a vintage short-sleeved black knit bolero jacket handed down to me from Grandma Mimi. It boasts an elaborate paisley pattern woven in golden thread. On the bottom: a black A-line skirt falling just above my knees, black tights, and knee-high black leather boots with a walkable heel.

My hair, boasting new blonde highlights and freshly trimmed bangs, falls to my shoulders. From my ears dangle gold teardrop-shaped hoop earrings, handed down from Mom. Around my neck is a gold-tone chain with a fourteen-carat Snoopy pendant I have had since childhood; the back of it has my name inscribed in cursive.

Once I am ready to change into an evening look, all I will have to do is apply some of the makeup that fills the bulging side pocket of my black leather purse. The fat black eyeliner there will give me the perfect retro raccoon eyes, and the pale-pink frosted Revlon lipstick will add authenticity.

That authenticity will impress my boyfriend Bill when I meet him later tonight outside the Ritz on East Eleventh Street in Manhattan. I am taking him out for his birthday to see Doctor and the Medics, the glam-rockers who have a hit in their native England with their version of the old Norman Greenbaum tune "Spirit in the Sky."

But to put on my makeup, I'll need to find a restroom, which is going to be a challenge, as I don't know my way around this cavernous old Newark church that goes by the strange name of St. Antoninus. And before I can find a restroom, I have to sit through the rest of this boring ceremony.

Jennifer is sitting next to me, dressed far more sensibly in a white peasant blouse and tan skirt. Mom is in a long white frilly dress, but to see her I have to bob my head over the tall person in front of me, as she is all the way up on the *bimah*, or whatever Catholics call the stage area by the altar.

The best I can make out is that right now an old priest in white robes is pouring water over Mom's head. That must be the one who's been teaching her Catholicism, Monsignor Oesterreicher.

I nudge Jennifer. "Isn't it great that Mom is finally settling into a normal religion?" She manages to suppress her giggle. Me, not so much.

About five hours later. Once again I am bobbing my head, trying to see around the person in front of me. This is my life.

Unfortunately, it is much harder to get a good sightline at the Ritz than it was at St. A's. Here, the man blocking my view is not only tall but also has tall hair—three inches of platinum spikes—and he too is bobbing his head, only he is doing it in time with the music.

At my side is Bill, resplendent in the vintage brocaded caftan I bought him—another birthday present. We have been together nearly nine weeks. That makes it the longest relationship I've ever had. Bill is two years older than me and publishes a mod fanzine, *Smashed Blocked*. He is just the kind of handsome, witty, musically aware boyfriend I have been dreaming of.

But Bill doesn't dream about me. A few days ago, he told me he had a dream about Liz, another girl from the Dive scene. And he said Liz likes him too, plus she just broke up with her boyfriend.

So this could be my last date with Bill. That is too much to think about right now.

Sometimes it helps to have loud live music and nightclub lights just to be distracted from my own thoughts. Tonight's music is not my favorite, but it is fun and mindless.

The bleached-blonde guitarist launches into a familiar fuzzed-out riff, sparking a cheer from the crowd. It's the one song they all know. Craning my neck, I catch sight of the singer prancing about, swishing his long brown hair like a corded whip.

"Prepare yourself, you know it's a must, gotta have a friend in Jesus . . ."

Oh, no. I forgot that when a band performs its hit at the Ritz, the technicians turn on the smoke machines for dramatic effect. It looks exciting from a distance but it is hard to take up close.

An acrid cloud arises, billowing pink and purple beneath

the stage lights, swallowing up the singer so that he seems to fade in and out of view.

"So you know that when you die he's gonna recommend you to the spirit in the sky . . ."

Cigarette smoke I can tune out, but not the chemical stuff emitted by the machines. Instinctively I rub my eyes. Before I can stop myself, half my eyeliner comes off onto my fingertips.

A quick glance into my makeup mirror confirms the damage has been done. I am a stained mess.

"I never sinned, I got a friend in Jesus . . ."

I mutter an obscenity under my breath. Five hundred people stand between me and the nearest source of water. There is no way I can get clean.

3 Soul and Inspiration

Thursday, October 30, 1986, 3:26 p.m. "It was in the city of shame / That I found I wasn't to blame . . ."

Robyn Hitchcock's "City of Shame" runs through my head as I briskly walk down Washington Square Park East, my newly-heeled black leather ankle boots making a satisfying tap on the pavement. I had just enough time after my afternoon class to dash back to my dorm to put on some makeup before trekking over to Tower Records for a performance and record-signing by the eccentric and enigmatic British singer.

The signing isn't until four, but I've got to be there by three-thirty to have any chance of seeing the stage. My boots don't add much height, plus I am probably not the only fan who wants to take in Hitchcock's good looks.

As I turn onto West Fourth Street, a young woman is trying to get the attention of passers-by. "Free Bible! Free Bible!"

I turn my head to size her up. She has straight brown hair and is wearing a kind of generic college-student outfit—a plain sweater and jeans. The look is definitely more Midwest than Manhattan. A cornfed hick out to convert pagans in Sin City.

"Would you like a Bible?" she asks. "It's free."

"Sure, thanks."

What the heck. Mom owns a Christian Bible; I might as well too. Anyhow, I can't resist a free book.

My answer is rewarded with a smile and a green volume small enough to fit into my hand, its leatherette cover bearing the gold-engraved legend *New Testament • Psalms • Proverbs*.

It's as if the Old Testament never happened. How like Christians to call something so truncated a "Bible"!

Thankfully the woman doesn't ask for anything in return, so I can keep walking toward Tower with my stride nearly unbroken. I stuff the bowdlerized Bible into my red leather pocketbook, where it will have to fight for breathing space with my Day-Timer calendar, ten or eleven lipsticks, and a retractable gold-toned metal case from Manic Panic containing a lip brush I hardly ever use.

My lipstick options include silvers, whites, and frosty nudes, along with the odd red, mauve, and magenta. And that's just what I have on hand; I have many more lipsticks at my dorm. I buy one whenever I need a pick-me-up, and I have been needing a lot of pick-me-ups lately, especially since Bill dumped me for Liz. Each time, I excuse the expenditure by telling myself that this is the perfect lipstick and that, once I start wearing it, I am not going to need another.

Before I know it, I'm inside the doors at Tower, aptly named given its four levels of records and cassettes. The main floor is about the size of a tennis court, crammed with long aisles of display racks. At its center, several large racks have been pushed aside to make room for a platform that will serve as the stage.

I spy a large display at the right side of the stage—my right, near the staircase leading to the mezzanine. It advertises the new album that Hitchcock and his band the Egyptians will be signing after their performance, *Element of Light*. The cover bears a black-and-white photo of Hitchcock sitting within the cleft of a rock, an electric guitar in his lap. His expression, introspective and inscrutable, reminds me of David Bowie minus the makeup.

My challenge is to squeeze into one of the aisles at an angle that will afford me a decent view. It's not easy when the place is already crowded with a hundred hip fans clad in almost as many shades of black. A few paisley, striped, or polka-dotted shirts break up the monotony.

I find a spot next to a rack displaying Bon Jovi's latest album—no one in this crowd will care that I'm blocking it—and stake my claim. It's about forty feet away from the stage, but at least I'll have a reasonably clear sightline if the leather-jacketed couple in front of me doesn't move around too much.

Looking toward the stage, I can make out a cocktail drum kit. There is also a roadie in a threadbare t-shirt and faded jeans. He is strumming a few bland chords on a black Gibson guitar and fiddling with the knobs of a small Fender amp.

My eyes are searching the crowd for familiar faces but I don't see anyone except Jack Rabid, editor of *The Big Takeover* fanzine, standing in his usual spot by the front, his cheekbones looking razor sharp in Tower's headache-inducing fluorescent lights. Considering how prominent Jack is on the scene—all the bands know him and he knows them—he is actually very humble and down-to-earth. If only I could squeeze my way through to where he is, he would let me stand in front of him. But I can't and anyway I hate being pressed against the stage.

Wish my *Jersey Beat* editor Jim Testa were here, but he's at his day job. Too bad. I wanted to get his thoughts on what I should ask the Smithereens when I interview them for *The Bob*. Jim's known them since the days when their biggest claim to fame was being the house band at New Jersey's Dirt Club. With his help, I could come up with some bright questions to distinguish me from the trendy critics who discovered them only after they made it onto MTV.

None of my schoolmates are in sight either, but that's no surprise. I didn't bother inviting any of them except my friend Kate, who is at her internship; I imagined the rest wouldn't be interested.

When I first started at NYU, I had hoped to find friends there. Isn't that what people are supposed to do at college? Instead, just as in high school, most of my friends are musicians and writers slightly older than me, burdened with day jobs. Nearly all are men. That in itself wouldn't be so bad. But it ends up making my life complicated because either they like me romantically or I like them, and it never seems to match up that we like each other that way at the same time.

One hour later. Hitchcock still looks every bit as crush-worthy and his absurdist wordplay is still every bit as charming as when I caught him at Maxwell's in Hoboken back in March. Between songs, he engages the audience with rapid-fire monologues—stream-of-consciousness tales concerning characters like customs agents, circus performers, and victims of bubonic plague who interact with wildly transmuted flora and fauna such as bees, sea creatures, and radishes.

I wish I could lose myself in Hitchcock's songs. It would be the next best thing to losing myself in him.

His melodies are so engaging, with that almost baroque quality that the best songwriters had in the Sixties, my favorite era for pop music. But when I try to get inside his lyrics, I hit a brick wall. Occasionally he draws a word picture that betrays something powerful going on beneath the surface of his mind—something deep and beautiful and sad. But then right away he changes the topic to fish eggs or bongos or something.

After playing a subdued number I don't recognize, Hitchcock asks if there are any requests. Suggestions erupt from all sides. Some guy in the front shouts for "Queen of Eyes" and I echo his cry as loudly as I can.

Hitchcock pauses for a brief moment and then strums some familiar chords that reverberate with a post-punk crackle. I screech my approval—it's "City of Shame"!

Hearing the song live, I can understand the words better than I could when listening to them on record. Gosh, they're dark.

It was in the City of Love
All the flesh I ate was never enough
Though I knew it wasn't good for my soul
My body hungered for the ultimate goal

Six minutes later. Hitchcock and members of his band, the Egyptians, have just finished singing "Uncorrected Personality Traits." Some woman in the front row waves one of his albums under his chin.

Hitchcock looks around from side to side and then down at the audience member. "I believe we are going to sign some records, but we can't right now. You see, we need a table . . ."

"I'll be a table!"

That is my voice. I cannot believe I just said that, or rather shouted it. And lifted up my hand at the same time as though I were bidding at an auction.

Hitchcock seems startled but quickly composes himself. He turns his head in my direction. "I believe we have a lady here who is offering to be a table?"

"Yes!" I exclaim with near-hysterical delight. "I'll be a table!"

He narrows his gaze with a kind of wonder. Our eye-beams cross. I babble on. "I'll get down onto my hands and knees, and you can sign albums on my back!"

The audience members in front are all looking over their shoulders at me. Several chuckle. There is a moment of extraordinarily awkward silence. Hitchcock begins to hem: "Well, uh . . ."

Just then a young man in a bright yellow Tower Records t-shirt dashes toward the stage and says something to Hitchcock.

"Ah," Hitchcock replies. He looks back over to me. "Thank you for your kind offer, but it does appear that we have a record-signing area over there"—he motions toward the display near the base of the staircase—"and they are bringing over a table. We'll just do one more song . . ."

Thankfully the crowd has turned back to face the stage. But I am looking down, astonished at myself.

Really, I should congratulate myself for having done the seemingly impossible. I have out-absurded Robyn Hitchcock! Yes, that's what I should do: put a positive spin on it, think about how brilliant and witty I am. Instead I'm feeling choked up and want to crawl under a rock.

As the crowd cheers the first few notes of Hitchcock's final tune, I seize my chance to slip out. I don't want to stay for the signing anyway. Why spend $8.99 for an album I'll never play?

Monday, May 11, 1987, 3:40 p.m. "Wow, Shane, I didn't know you were a fan of Liberace!"

A newspaper photo of the flamboyant pianist and recent AIDS casualty adorns the side of a tall gray steel filing cabinet beside my friend's desk. As I lean down for a better look, I see that the clipping is crammed alongside ones depicting a host of other celebrities: Andy Warhol, Benny Goodman, Danny Kaye, Rick Nelson . . . Each one is sealed to the cabinet with an ominous-looking border of black duct tape.

I look over to where Shane is seated at his desk. His face softens into a sheepish smile.

It's my first time visiting Shane at the printing house where he works in the Meatpacking District, an industrial wasteland on the western edge of lower Manhattan. Normally our paths cross at clubs where he performs with his band the Cheepskates; a couple of times, he's had me over to visit at his home in Brooklyn and take in his amazing record collection. I wish we saw each other more often, but—although I know he would like to have a girlfriend—he has politely made it clear that we are just friends. Maybe he is put off by the fact that I am only eighteen and he is in his early thirties, although I have found that most men don't care about such things.

"That's the Wall of Death," Shane explains.

"Wall of Death?"

"A co-worker started it. Whenever a celebrity dies, one of us adds his picture to the wall."

"Ah."

Shane reaches between some piles of papers on his desk and pulls out a cassette. "Here you are."

It was for the sake of picking up this tape before returning home for the summer that I made the twenty-minute walk from my dorm. I take it eagerly and read Shane's writing on the cover. Side A is by Curt Boettcher's studio group Sagittarius, including their debut album *Present Tense*, and Side B is Boettcher's solo album *There's an Innocent Face*.

"It's just what I wanted! Thank you so much!"

"There was extra space on Side A, so after *Present Tense* I added some songs from Sagittarius's second album. I didn't think you'd want the whole thing, because Curt doesn't seem to have been as involved with it as he was with the first album, and it's not as good."

"That's great! I'm sure I'll love it. Thanks for using a chrome-bias tape too."

Shane shrugs, muttering "of course" as he pulls out a cigarette from a box of Camels and lights it.

When will I learn not to be so gushy with him? It only puts him off.

"I hate to see you smoke. It's bad for your voice."

His singing is so gorgeous, like a sweeter-sounding Neil Young. He has brown eyes like Neil's too.

Shane pauses a moment before answering, turning his head away from me to exhale. "Well, Nat King Cole smoked like a chimney and he never lost his voice. He kept sounding better and better until he died of lung cancer."

All I can manage in response is an incredulous "really!" Something about Shane's logic must be off, but it's no use arguing the point; the only tune I know by Cole is "The Christmas Song."

Eight minutes later. Walking down Fourteenth Street toward my dorm and trying not to think about how I wish Shane wanted me. What I should be thinking about is his kindness in taping me music from his collection, as he has done many times during the year and a half that we've been friends.

How long ago was it that I visited Shane at home for the first time and he turned me on to Curt Boettcher? It must have been over a year ago because I remember how annoyed I was last spring when I was falling asleep listening to the Millennium's album on headphones and my roommate turned down the volume knob to inform me I was snoring.

What I do remember is sitting on the well-worn couch in Shane's living room. The room seemed narrower than it actually was because the opposite wall housed his stereo and speakers as well as LP records tightly packed on floor-to-ceiling rows of shelves. Many of the records were passed on to Shane from his father, who collected them during his career as a disc jockey in the tiny upstate town of Malone, N.Y.

I remember how Shane positioned himself at a safe distance, his back to me as he ran his fingers through the albums to find obscure gems to spin on his audiophile-quality turntable.

After introducing me to some artists from the early Seventies—the Wombles, Blue Ash, and one that was simply called Blue—Shane showed me a late-Sixties album I had never seen by a group I had never heard of. They were called the Millennium and the album had the hopeful title *Begin*. Its front cover was taken up with a simple medieval-style woodcut depicting a pastoral landscape with a fruit tree, two doves, puffy clouds, and, on the horizon, a church emanating sunlike rays. On the back was a black-and-white photo of seven clean-shaven, modish, intelligent-looking young men.

"Their look reminds me of the Association," I said.

"Well, that's probably no coincidence," Shane replied, taking the album back from me and pulling the disc out of its sleeve. "Their co-producer, Curt Boettcher—the one in the ruffled collar—also produced the Association's first album, the one with 'Along Comes Mary' and 'Cherish.'"

"Really! Do they sound like the Association?"

"Sort of. Not exactly."

He placed the album on the turntable.

"They do some interesting things with stereo, so you might want to listen between the speakers."

I obligingly took a cushion off the couch, placed it on the rug between the speakers, and lay down on my back.

"This song's called 'It's You,'" Shane said as he gingerly let down the needle at the beginning of side 2.

He then stepped aside to put extra space between himself and my supine figure. In retrospect he needn't have done so. A moment later, I was hardly aware he was even there.

It is hard to describe what happened. I just remember being utterly transported.

The record didn't sound like something recorded in 1968. It sounded as though it were coming from the future. There were familiar Sixties elements, to be sure: ringing acoustic guitars and layered vocal harmonies that I knew from West Coast artists such as the Byrds or the Beach Boys. The composition itself had a lovely, plaintive melody. Save for its lyrics, which were mysterious and slightly unnerving, it could almost pass for a folk-rock love song, like the Lovin' Spoonful's "Darling Be Home Soon." But the production and arrangement were unlike anything I had ever heard.

Can ears shift perspective the way eyes do? As a child I was fascinated with optical illusions like the silhouetted vase that can also be seen as two faces in profile. Lying on Shane's floor with closed eyes listening to "It's You" that first time, I had the mind-bending impression that the record was offering me the choice between perceiving it as an organic whole or as a painstakingly constructed mosaic of differentiated parts.

How is it possible for something to be so perfectly calculated and yet so authentically affecting? It was like the

musical equivalent of those Impressionist paintings that
look from a distance as though they are painted the usual
way, but when you get up close you find they are actually
thousands of tiny dots. My ears went back and forth between both perspectives—the wide view and the close-up
view—until my senses were overloaded and I was utterly
bedazzled.

There was something else about the song too, something
that I am even less capable of putting into words. Through it
all, there was beauty combined with a nagging anxiety and
what I can only describe as an overwhelming sadness. It was
like my heart writ large. I wanted to get inside the record,
to live inside it. And I wanted to know the people who created it—especially Boettcher, whom Shane identified as the
album's mastermind.

Shane showed me the other Boettcher albums in his collection—the Sagittarius LPs and *There's an Innocent Face*. The
front cover of the solo album was taken up with a photograph of Curt's beatific-looking face, airbrushed to the point
that he looked like a storybook angel.

"There's something about his expression," Shane ob-
served hesitatingly. "I don't know, but I just have the feeling
he might be gay."

I took a second look at the cover and agreed disappoint-
edly that Shane was likely on the mark.

"How does it sound? I asked. "Is it like the Millennium?"

"No, not really. It's very good, but it's different. It doesn't
have the same kinds of vocal arrangements you hear on the
Millennium album. Some of the songs have a country feel."

"Oh. Then I won't ask you to tape it for me. But I'd love
it if you'd tape me the Millennium!"

"I might be able to do better than that. Let me see what
I have."

Shane disappeared into another room and returned with a 45 as well as another copy of the Millennium album. I saw with delight that the single was a DJ copy of "It's You," complete with a picture sleeve featuring a beautiful black-and-white photo of the group, different from the one on their album cover.

"My dad received this 45 at the radio station back when it came out," Shane said. "And I have this extra copy of the album. Pick whichever one you want and it's yours."

I squealed some words of gratitude and then paused to deliberate. The single was appealing because, given how rare the album was, a DJ 45 from it with an intact picture sleeve was likely to be even rarer. Also, I had a special love for 45s and had just started publishing a one-sheet 'zine about them, *7 inches*. But given that both the songs from the single were on the album, it would be pretty dumb to take just two songs when I could have fourteen . . .

The sight of the guard at NYU's Weinstein Hall dormitory jolts me back to the present moment. I show him my ID and head up to my room to play the Boettcher cassette Shane gave me. Hope my roommate isn't studying so I can listen without headphones.

With the Millennium album being burned into my soul, it is thrilling to have a whole new world of Boettcher music to discover. I may not ever have Shane. But I will always have Curt.

Wednesday, June 10, 1987, 4:10 p.m. Sitting on the brown couch in what I once knew as Grandma Jessie and Grandpa Buddy's house in Millburn, N.J. Mom and I moved here after Grandpa died last year and are living here until the house sells, which will probably be soon. At least, I hope it is, as I can't stand how Mom is on my back to keep the house immaculate in advance of potential buyers coming to view it. Last night she actually woke me up and threatened all kinds of penalties unless I washed two dishes I'd left in the kitchen sink.

Just as with last year, the beginning of summer is the worst. My social life has suddenly ground to a halt. Yes, it's great not to have classes, but now I am stuck here in suburbia until fall comes and I can return to my dorm.

I do make it into the city most days, either to work at my publicity gig for Tramps nightclub or just to get away. But the train is expensive, plus Mom complains at having to drive me to the station, even though it only takes her slightly out of her way to work. Worst of all, just as in high school, the train schedule prevents me from going to shows in the city. Mom keeps trying to get me to learn to drive, but I tell her my lazy eye makes it impossible, as I can't see depth or judge distances. The world is a safer place without me behind a wheel.

On the upside, having time at home enables me to catch up on my listening pile. Ever since I began writing for *The Bob*, independent labels and artists have been sending me review copies of their records. Most of them are mediocre, but once in a while there is a real gem.

Right now, the album at the top of the pile is *Batteries Not Included* by Hysteric Narcotics. But I am feeling down and would rather listen to the tape Shane made me of Sagittarius and Curt Boettcher.

I don't trust Grandma and Grandpa's old stereo—its worn-out tape heads might eat up my cassette—so I bring my boom box down from my bedroom and pop in side A of the tape to hear Sagitarrius's *Present Tense*. Out wafts the sound of finger-picked guitar swirls descending gently like a Bach fugue. Curt sings hauntingly of "another time" when the listener will return his love.

This music is every bit as good as classics of the era like the Beach Boys' *Pet Sounds* or the Left Banke's albums. Why has another time never arrived for Curt? Why am I the only one among my music-loving friends, apart from Shane, who recognizes his name?

Another thought occurs, the same one that comes whenever I listen to the Millennium. My knowledge of Curt ends fifteen years ago with the release of his solo album. What happened to him afterward? Did he stay in music? Does he have other phenomenal records I've never heard about? Why don't I track him down and interview him for *The Bob* like I did with the Left Banke? Or maybe I could convince *Goldmine* magazine editor Jeff Tamarkin to run the interview. Then thousands of record collectors would learn about this forgotten genius.

Perhaps Curt's number is listed? But how would I find out? Even if he is still in Los Angeles, it's not as easy as one might think to find a number by dialing Information. If I dialed the area code and 555-1212, the operator would make me choose three municipalities to search, and if they all came up blank, I would still have to pay the $1.50 toll. My best option would be to find a library that keeps phone books from around the country. It would be a hassle, but I could do it.

Now the fears are coming up—the same one that prevented me from tracking down Curt the last time I thought of doing so. What if I were to reach him only to have him hang up on me? Or what if he turned out to be a bitter and burned-out shadow of his former self? I would be crushed. And I know that's not a far-fetched possibility. Some of the Left Banke members I interviewed were burned out, and my memory of them affects the way I hear their music now. I can no longer appreciate its innocence and joy as I did before. What was once unqualifiedly beautiful now sounds ironic and sad.

As I roll over the possible scenarios in my mind, the cassette spools on. Another wistful love song comes up. Curt's impossibly pure voice, sounding every bit as angelic as that ethereal photo on his solo-album cover looks, asks the object of his affection if she—he?—will ever know how he feels. Again he is reaching out toward a love of seemingly cosmic dimensions. The sense of longing is so intense, I can hardly bear it.

What if I am wrong about Curt's being burned out? What if he has happy memories about his music-making years and wants to share them? Given the quality of his work, wouldn't it be a crime not to take the chance and reach out to let him know he hasn't been forgotten?

My conscience won't let me rest until I come up with an action plan. I decide to call an expert on West Coast music of the 1960s to find out if he has any word on whether Curt is reachable.

Greg Shaw, an accomplished rock historian and head of Bomp! Records, is the obvious choice. We've never spoken, but he knows the editors of the 'zines I write for, and he's probably read my writings. I call Jim Testa for Greg's number; armed with it, I call using Grandma and Grandpa's black rotary phone. Mom won't be happy that I'm calling long distance, but I'll worry about that when the bill comes in.

The voice on the other end sounds exactly as I'd imagined. Greg has a laid-back California accent and phrasing, but his mind is sharp and his musical knowledge is encyclopedic. He recognizes my name and is happy to help, but he hasn't heard any news of Curt in several years and can't think of anyone who has.

I sigh. Maybe there is one last hope.

"Was he still living in LA when you last heard of him? Maybe I could find him in the phone book."

Greg laughs. "He's not going to be in the phone book."

"How do you know?"

"You don't know LA. Nobody who's anybody is in the phone book here. *Nobody.*"

"Really?"

"No one in the entertainment business. I'm telling you, the only people you're going to find in the LA phone book are people named Gomez."

I give up.

Monday, August 24, 1987, 9:37 p.m. Finally! Back in my own bedroom where I can be alone with my thoughts.

Mom did me a favor in picking me up from the airport, but she always wants to know everything. All through the ride home, as she was quizzing me on whether Gary was everything I had hoped he would be, I wished I could just keep my memories of him to myself and not have to share them.

As I take off my shoes, an improbable quantity of sand falls out. At least there is one memory I can keep to myself. Mom doesn't know that Gary and I kissed on a moonlit beach and I have no intention of telling her about it, even though it wouldn't scandalize her in the least. I will never forget that night, just as I will never forget June 14 of this year—the day Gary wrote his first letter to me.

That reminds me: after I get some sleep, I must write to Dave Klassen to thank him for introducing me to Gary. Looking back, it's hard to believe how, two years ago, having made Dave the object of my latest unrequited crush, I was so broken up when he moved to Toronto. If I had known he would reconnect there with his former bandmate Gary and give him my address, I would have celebrated.

When I read Gary's first letter, penned in that impossibly neat handwriting, I could hardly believe that this fantastic creature existed, let alone that he approached me rather than vice versa. A rock historian and fanzine publisher who was not only a singer, guitarist, and songwriter but also made an actual living playing in a band—it was as though my ideal boyfriend had jumped out of my fantasies and into real life.

Granted, Gary's money-making group was a Beach Boys clone band; his stage name was Gary Jardine. But still, he was gainfully employed and, as far as I could tell from a distance, wasn't blowing his money on any substances more mind-altering than Everly Brothers reissues. Plus he read real literature, not just rock magazines or murder mysteries. For fun, he wrote satirical essays that read like John Lennon's imitations of James Joyce.

Over the next three months, Gary and I exchanged letters practically every week, inserting them into packages crammed with music-related goodies and memorabilia—cassettes, fanzines, news clippings, ticket stubs, guitar picks . . .

We also exchanged photos of ourselves, though I sent many more than he did. With his pensive face and nondescript clothes, he looked more like an English Lit professor than a rocker. Still, I had a feeling that if I met him, I would fall in love.

And so I asked dear Dave if I could come stay at his place for a long weekend, explaining in all honesty that it was a pretext for meeting Gary. And I did. And now I am in love.

Wish I knew if Gary feels the same.

He wanted to be alone with me. That much I know. It was his idea to take the ferry to Toronto Island. Then I thought of bringing dinner so we could have a picnic as the sun went down. I didn't know we would be the only ones left on the beach to gaze at the city across the harbor, watching the lights of small planes glide over the water like shooting stars.

As we sat together on a towel in the sand, just when I thought there was no chance of his ever wanting me, he turned to me, held my gaze, and without a word brought his lips to mine.

This is the most romantic moment of my whole life, I thought. *I can't spoil this. It has to be perfect.* But I could spoil it if I put my whole body up against Gary's. Then it would just be like any other affair. I might be a virgin, but I knew what it was like to try to get as much as I could out of a man in one night for fear it would be my only chance with him. It couldn't be like that with Gary. If the first night I kissed him was also the last, I would have nothing left to live for.

So Gary and I fell to the sand, kissing and nuzzling, he on his back, me on my stomach, my body at an angle to his, my hips carving a crevice in the sand. And a familiar song kept going through my head, only I couldn't remember where I had heard it before.

Gary would know. "What's that song," I asked, "that song that goes, 'Been so long since I held you'?"

"It sounds familiar," he said softly. "But I don't know."

Then all too soon we had to dust ourselves off and run to catch the ferry and then the subway back to Dave's apartment.

Gary was too shy to kiss or hug me goodbye in front of Dave. It was like nothing had happened between us. Surely he could tell I wanted him to say some word, something to give me hope, to make me feel like we had made a beginning. But all I got was a wish for safe travels home. And throughout my waking hours from that moment last night until now as I take a damp paper towel to mop the sand off the rug so Mom doesn't get mad, that same song has kept going through my head.

"Been so long since I held you . . ." The melody sounds like it's from the Seventies. But what music do I have that's from the Seventies? It's not Big Star. Maybe it's from Curt Boettcher's solo album? I've hardly listened to that side of the cassette Shane made for me, since the Sagittarius side sounds more like the Millennium album that I so adore.

I put the Boettcher cassette into my boom box, turning down the volume so as not to disturb Mom. The first song, "I Love You More Each Day," announces its arrival with two—three?—acoustic guitars striking a wistful minor chord.

And there it is, that wonderful chorus: "Been so long since I held you."

I've had this tape of Curt's solo album for four months. How could I not have realized how good it is? Now I have to listen to the whole album before I go to bed—*really* listen to it, appreciating it for what it is and not for what I hoped it would be. I just know I'll fall in love.

4 I Had Too Much
to Dream Last Night

Wednesday, October 7, 1987, 7:37 p.m. "Signs, signs, everywhere a sign."

There is good reason why that hippie classic by Five Man Electrical Band is running through my head as I sit in my dorm room sipping a stale Diet Pepsi. I have to write a stupid paper for my Language, Thought, and Culture class on a section of Susanne Langer's *Philosophy in a New Key* concerning signs versus symbols. Specifically, I am supposed to give an example of how a picture may be considered a symbol. Thankfully, Dr. Nystrom only wants one page, but I can't believe she thinks it takes more than two sentences to explain something so simple.

If only I had done the smart thing and majored in journalism, I would have exciting class assignments instead of this busywork. But no, I wanted so badly to work at a major label that I had to enter the music-business program, even though I could do neither music nor business. It's amazing that I made it through two years there.

By the time I failed accounting for the second semester in a row and got a D in piano class, it was too late to enter the journalism program if I wanted to graduate on time. My adviser suggested I switch to the communications program instead. Great, I thought, I'll learn how to communicate with people via radio, TV, and public speaking.

But no, I had to wind up in "the country's premier media-ecology program." This is my fifth week in it and I'll be darned if I know what media ecology is. All I can tell is that it isn't media, it isn't ecology, and it isn't much fun.

That's not to say Dr. Nystrom is a bad professor. She's clearly super smart, and she puts her heart into teaching. I just don't understand why she's making us parse out the differences between signs and symbols. Who cares? I mean, why does anyone need to study what signs or symbols are? They just *are*, that's all.

But, like it or not, I have to do the assignment, otherwise I'll be embarrassed tomorrow morning if Dr. Nystrom notices I didn't turn it in.

So! An example of a picture that is a symbol! What would that be? It can't be that hard . . .

I've got it. It'll be good and morbid, which is what Dr. Nystrom deserves for giving me this lame assignment. No, I don't mean that. She hasn't done me any wrong. I'm just feeling another depression coming on and I'm scared. And I can't call Gary because he's on the road with Endless Summer; besides, it's too depressing speaking with him when he acts as though nothing special passed between us. The most he's let on about what he thinks of me was that vague aside in a letter where he said I should "read between the lines." What that meant, I have no idea. He's desirable and I'm not, and he has the power to keep me hanging on. I gave him that power and something deep inside me is incapable of taking it back. There is a black hole where my self-image should be.

My bed is a good place to write, thanks to the lap desk my stepmother gave me. I lean my back against the cinder-block wall, place my spiral notebook atop the lap desk, and scrawl out a draft. It takes me about half an hour.

Then I move to my desk and put a sheet of paper in the mammoth typewriter I inherited from Grandpa Buddy. Judging by its design, it looks to come from the same period as the '57 Chevy. Its gargantuan bulk is softened by sleek curves and a raised silver-toned Remington logo running across the front in cursive script.

I am the only student I know who uses one of these monsters. Others use either electric typewriters or word processors. But I wouldn't have it any other way. Retro is beautiful.

As I finish typing the paper, I can still smell the Liquid Paper I dabbed onto it to neaten up some errors. At least it looks clean. Better reread it to make sure I didn't miss any typos:

Every summer from 1976, when I was seven, through 1978, my mother sent me to the Greene Family Camp, a Jewish camp in Bruceville, Texas. The camp management had a group photo taken every year showing all the campers and counselors, and each of us would get a copy to take home. I would put mine on the stucco wall of my bedroom, where my mom let me use thumbtacks to hold up my posters.

At some point—I think it was after the 1978 photo—I was feeling really sad and hating myself. So I got the idea of taking one of the thumbtacks and putting it through my face in the photo. Now a dull circle of metal was where my face should be. It was a risky thing to do because it would have worried Mom if she saw it, plus she would have been mad that I ruined a picture of myself. I think it was a cry for help. But no one ever noticed it.

After a while, I got bolder and would stick the tack in and out, putting it in various parts of my face. Sometimes I would leave the tack off the photo and there would just be the holess. It felt weird and kind of scary to do it, not that I was superstitious, but just that it was a symbol of me. But the symbolism expressed how I felt about myself—my sadness, my frustration, my low self-image.

Darn. An extra "s" in "holes." I don't feel like retyping, so I'll just use my pen to make a slash through it.

The ending could be better; it just trails off. But I'm going to leave it as is because I'm doing what the assignment asked. It fills a page, it's good enough for a passing grade, and I have no desire to spend any more time on it. My depression is catching up with me and right now all I want to do is go to the Korean deli, buy three dollars' worth of chocolate-coated rum balls and a fresh Diet Pepsi, and listen to the tape Shane made me of *Big Star Third*.

Thursday, October 15, 1987, 11 a.m. At last, the bell! Just in time too, as I ran out of ideas of things to doodle and records to add to my wish list during today's Language, Thought, and Culture class.

As I grab my notebook to leave, Dr. Nystrom approaches me.

"Dawn, could I see you for a moment?"

"Sure!" I exclaim, a little too brightly.

My heart pounds and I get a sinking feeling in my stomach. Why did I write that paper when I knew it would expose me as suicidal?

Maybe it was a cry for help.

Yes. On some level, I want Dr. Nystrom to call the administration, and the administration to call my mother, and my mother to call a psychiatrist, and the psychiatrist to call my dad, and everyone to feel very sad about me.

But what's more likely is that I will feel terrible about causing my mother more grief and there will be no way I can stop hurting her or anyone who cares about me unless I kill myself. Then they will all feel bad for a while but they will eventually forget me and go on with their lives. And if they don't forget me, it doesn't really matter because sooner or later everyone dies.

I walk around the students' desks, which are arranged like a rectangle with one of the short sides missing, and make it over toward Dr. Nystrom as she stands by the teacher's desk.

Dr. Nystrom picks up a pen from the desk and rolls it absently between her fingers. If she weren't talking with me, she would be having her post-class Marlboro right now with her colleague Dr. Neil Postman. I hope she doesn't ask me to comment on the book of his that I was supposed to have read for today's class: *Amusing Ourselves to Death*. And I hope even more that she didn't find out I joked to the other students after class last week that it should be called *Smoking Ourselves to Death*.

"Dawn," she says with an air of gravity.

I shift a bit and glance at the floor. Out with it, Dr. Nystrom. Yes, I am messed up. Yes, I need help. You're concerned. Just say it.

"Your reflection was *remarkable*."

I look up and find to my surprise that she is not looking at me with concern. She is looking at me with admiration.

"The example you gave was so *creative*. I could just *picture* how you used that thumbtack on the photograph to express your *feelings* about yourself. It's such a *perfect* way to capture the symbolic value of a picture. Really, it was *profound*."

"Uh, wow!" I reply, forcing a smile. "Really! Thank you. I wasn't expecting that."

"I would like to read it to the class on Monday so that I might discuss what it brings out that's relevant to what we have been reading in Langer. Would that be all right?"

"Oh, sure! I'd be honored. Thank you."

"Thank *you*."

I exit into the hall and find my way to the women's room—not the new one, but the small old one that hardly anyone uses. My face feels hot from holding everything in and I don't want anyone to see me cry.

I tore my heart out to fulfill a stupid assignment and all Dr. Nystrom saw was a laboratory specimen. She doesn't care. She really doesn't care. Just like the world.

Thursday, November 19, 1987, 11:53 p.m. My roommate has already gone to her parents for the weekend, which is great, because it means that, among other things, I can fall asleep to music without having to put on my clunky Radio Shack padded headphones.

I pop the cassette I made of the Millennium's album into my stereo—having it on tape enables me to avoid wearing down my copy of the valuable LP—and get under the covers.

Sleep won't come easily at the end of a day when I enjoyed three Diet Pepsis. It's also hard to calm down because Gary's latest package arrived today. It was stocked with the usual fascinating memorabilia and carefully curated cassette of vintage pop. But what really excited me was the accompanying letter, which, although characteristically cryptic, contained a number of references that might kinda sorta mean I'm almost nearly special to him. It's something to hold on to, anyway. And I need something to hold onto if I'm to want to wake up in the morning.

The last Millennium song to reach my ears before sleep arrives is "The Island." With its hypnotically repetitive acoustic-guitar figures, I would have thought it was an effort to imitate the Beatles' "Dear Prudence" or "Across the Universe." But I looked up the release dates and found that the Millennium's album actually came out before either of those songs.

In Curt's world, "The Island" is a mystical metaphor for something within; I'm not sure what.

"The Island is calling . . ." he sings. "It's saying you've got to let me out of this mental cage that we live in / It's time to free yourself and start to live instead of thinking about dying."

Curt's words echo in my mind as I drift into a sea of dreams . . .

Friday, November 20, 1987, 9:04 a.m. There is a thought in my head before I wake up. I arrive at consciousness to find it already there. Actually, it is not so much a thought as a certainty, a simple fact, a decision that has already been made:

I have to call Jeff Tamarkin and ask if he would be willing to run an interview with Curt Boettcher in Goldmine.

There is no longer any question in my mind that I have to interview Curt. There is no more deliberation. The decision came between when I fell asleep and when I woke up. I just have to interview him. It is a duty. How could I ever have thought otherwise? The world just has to know about his music, and I am going to be the one to tell them.

But I need one thing before I can begin—some sort of official sanction so that when I reach Curt, I can legitimately tell him that I have an outlet that is willing to publish my interview with him. It would be terrible to get his hopes up for nothing.

I punch in Jeff's number from memory. He picks up; I sigh with relief. There's no time to lose.

When I explain my request, Jeff admits that he knows of Curt only vaguely. He owns the Association album that Curt produced, he's familiar with Sagittarius through their minor hit "My World Fell Down," which was recorded before Curt joined the project, and he's aware that Curt worked briefly with the Beach Boys. But he knows that *Goldmine* readers will be interested, and that's what counts. So, yes, he says, go ahead.

Victory! But now I have to actually find Curt. Will have to get to work phoning friends, editors, anyone who might know someone who knows someone. Probably my best chance is to find a Beach Boys obsessive . . .

Monday, December 14, 1987, 5:27 p.m. Back at Mom's for Christmas vacation. Sitting at the telephone table by the bay window, where Grandma Jessie used to watch her bird feeder, I look out at the night sky. I should be feeling hopeful right now, for I am so close to finding Curt.

During the past three and a half weeks, Shane put me in touch with Boettcher collector Erik Lindgren; Erik in turn connected me with Fran Kowalski, who had conversations with Curt several years ago; and Fran helped me find Domenic Priore, a Los Angeles historian who got to know Curt in 1984.

The trail grew warmer when Domenic remembered the name of the recording studio where Curt worked, Valley Center Studios in Van Nuys. He saved me a call to Information by looking up the studio's number in the phone book.

But Domenic also told me something else, something that has me worried. He heard from someone, somewhere—he can't remember who—that Curt had died. But it could be false, especially if the rumors are true that Curt was gay. Nowadays when a famous gay man disappears from public view, it's common for people to jump to the conclusion that he died of AIDS.

If Curt did die, wouldn't his death have been reported? I checked with Jeff Tamarkin, who reads obituaries as part of his job for *Goldmine*, and he assured me he hadn't seen anything. Although Curt was by no means a household name, he was far more famous than half the people whose obituaries run in *Billboard*. It just doesn't make sense that Curt's death wouldn't merit a mention there or in any other industry journal. So I am skeptical, but still worried.

I take a deep breath, pick up the ancient phone's clunky black receiver, and dial the number I scrawled on one of Grandpa Buddy's old legal pads. It contains a zero and a bunch of eights and nines, so I hear about a hundred clicks on the line before the call finally goes through.

"Valley Center Studios. This is Mark."

My heart is beating fast. "Hi, Mark, my name is Dawn Eden and I'm a writer for *Goldmine* magazine. I wonder if you could help me. I'm interested in writing an article about Curt Boettcher and I heard he worked for you."

"He did. He died, you know."

Something inside me dies.

I take a breath. "Oh, I'm so sorry. I had heard a rumor, but I didn't know for sure. When was it?"

"Back in June, I think? I'll switch you over to our engineer, Dave Jenkins. He'll know."

Fifty minutes later. I return the receiver to its cradle. Mom's not yet home from work, which is good because I need to be alone with my thoughts as I review the conversation in my head.

I can't believe Curt died on June 14 of *this year*. So I missed him by exactly six months.

The circumstances of his death that Jenkins related to me were tragic, reminding me of what happened to Warhol in his final days. Curt entered the hospital suffering from pneumonia and went under the knife for what was supposed to be a routine biopsy, but something went terribly wrong. He was forty-three.

Jenkins also provided a window into what Curt had left behind: a wide circle of musical collaborators and friends. Although Curt was active in the gay subculture, he had once been married and fathered a son, now nineteen. I feel awful for that young man somewhere who is my age and has lost his dad.

"It's a shame you didn't know him," the engineer said to me. "He would have loved talking with you about his music and having you write about him. It would have made him so happy to be remembered"

"Well, then, I have to write about him anyway," I replied. "Only now I'll write a book."

I said that without thinking, but I really meant it. Writing a book on Curt was the most obvious thing to do. An article alone wouldn't serve to interest readers in a virtually unknown artist. However, a book could, because it would put Curt's life in the context of the larger musical worlds through which he moved.

But that's not the only reason I have to write a book. Undertaking it will enable me to move through Curt's world, to immerse myself in it. I love him too much to let death get in the way of my knowing him.

Perhaps, too, seeking out people who knew Curt, hunting down every last bit of information on his life and music, and telling the world about him will delay my death a bit longer. I can't die if I am the only one who can tell his story.

Thursday, February 16, 1989, 8:46 p.m.
Doesn't it always happen! I finally get into my favorite sitting position upon my bed, with the flat pillow under my back against the wall of my dorm room—a single one at last, after three years of roommates—and crack open my copy of Hans Christian Andersen's fairy tales to find one I haven't read, when the phone rings. I jump up, hit the stop button on my cassette deck so the caller doesn't hear Tommy Roe's *It's Now Winter's Day*, and pick up the receiver.

"Hello."

"Hello, Dawn? This is Gary Selman."

I roll my eyes. "Oh, hi, Gary." Just the Gary I did *not* want to hear from.

Selman is co-founder of Beth Israel, the Messianic Jewish "temple" (really, a church) that Mom started attending last year, and he co-hosts a call-in radio show with its pastor Jonathan Cahn. Like everyone at Beth Israel, he believes that "Yeshua" (Jesus' Hebrew name) is the Jewish Messiah.

Mom's basically thrown herself into Beth Israel's life. Its services use some of the Jewish prayers she remembers, and she has found a community there that she didn't have at St. A's.

I get it. I mean, I understand why a Jew who accepts Jesus would be put off by stuffy old white-bread Christianity and long for the earthiness of Jewish ritual practice. When I see Christians on TV—which, here in Greenwich Village, is practically the only place I see them—everything about them seems artificial, from their overly sprayed hair, to their polyester clothes, to the sappy hymns that they force through their toothpaste-commercial smiles. So I can appreciate that a Jewish convert to Christianity would not want to have to give up Hebrew chanting and Shabbat candles and challah and Torah and self-deprecating jokes and being able to kvetch once in a while.

But just because I appreciate the Jewish approach to Christianity better than the Christian approach doesn't mean I want to be a Messianic Jew. It's all right for Mom because she really feels it. Jesus is real to her. But when I went with her to Beth Israel one Friday night several weeks ago—partly to please her and partly because I really wished for the happiness she's found in her faith—I wasn't feeling it.

For one thing, the whole atmosphere of Beth Israel put me off. It's the kind of place where everybody hugs each other, and I hate feeling pressured to let someone hug me that I don't even know.

Mom, however, is the queen of hugs. She's there for everyone, especially those who are mentally disturbed and/or smelly. When I visited Beth Israel, all those people ran to her when they saw her, and then she passed them all on to me, proud to have them meet her daughter.

For another thing, I couldn't stand most of the music; the songs were dull and repetitive, and they went on and on. There were no songbooks; people just stood and read lyrics off a projection screen:

OUR GOD IS AN AWESOME GOD
OUR GOD IS AN AWESOME GOD
OUR GOD IS AN AWESOME GOD
(REPEAT 3X)

Thankfully, the singing eventually had to pause for Bible readings and Pastor Jonathan's sermon, which likewise went on too long but at least was interesting. I liked how he delved into the meaning of different Hebrew words in the Old Testament.

But then came more singing. As the tempo picked up, with worshipers following the projected instructions to sing various combinations of "PRAISE" and "HOLY" and "YOU ARE WORTHY," I felt an overwhelming sense of loneliness.

Everybody else was feeling the spirit of the worship, just like Mom does. They were all sharing in the feeling that God loved them, God cared about them, Jesus was real, and life had meaning. They all were high on Jesus. And me? I was just clapping along and trying not to look like I wished I were anywhere but there.

It was like "The Emperor's New Clothes," but in reverse. Something, someone was really present to all those people smiling and clapping around me. It had to be; I'm not so cynical as to believe that every joyful religious person everywhere in the world is deluded or faking it. And I wanted to believe; I really did. I even made a silent prayer I learned as a child from a book of Jewish wisdom—praying that I might pray well. But that something or someone clearly wanted nothing to do with me.

And now Beth Israel's own Gary Selman is on the line. I remember with regret that Mom asked me if she could give him my number so he could talk to me about Yeshua. This man isn't calling because he wants to know me. He is calling because he wants to convert me.

Mom meant well. She knew I was hurting and she wanted me to share in the happiness that she has. Practically all her spare time is taken up with volunteering at Beth Israel, where she gives classes in Hebrew and in Jewish dance. Given all she does for me, the least I can do is give Selman an hour of my time.

Selman sounds on the phone like he does on the radio— aggressively friendly and sure of himself. I instinctively bristle as I do whenever someone tries to hard-sell me on something. He senses this and tries to come back with wit, but his tone strikes me as forced.

Within the first few minutes of the conversation it becomes clear that Selman is trying to identify my weak spot. He is intrigued by my admission that I have read the Gospels and have no real objection to Jesus.

I wish Jesus was the Messiah. But I don't feel anything when I read the Gospels, or any part of the Bible, for that matter; it's just words on a page. And when I go to a service at a church or temple, there's nothing for me to hold on to. I might think God is near me for a moment when I say a prayer or sing a song. But then I return to my everyday life and the sense of God evaporates. If God really loved me, wouldn't he be with me all the time?

Selman responds that God *will* be with me all the time—if I pray in Jesus' name. But if I don't pray in Jesus' name, God won't hear me. When I object—doesn't God know everything?—he clarifies: God *will* hear the prayers of those who don't call upon Jesus, but he won't answer them.

I am repulsed at the implication that God doesn't hear Jews' prayers, and I push back: Doesn't God hear the prayers of good people? But Selman digs in his heels. It doesn't matter how "good" people are, he says. If they don't accept Yeshua as their Lord and Savior, they are going to hell.

Now I am really disturbed. "If what you're telling me is true, then my Grandma Jessie, who was the most saintly person I have ever known, is right now burning in hell.

"Is that what you're saying?" I press on. "Are you saying that my mother's mother, my Grandma Jessie, is at this moment burning in hell?"

"If she didn't accept Yeshua, then yes."

I am utterly disgusted. "It's getting late. I have to go."

"Wait, before you go, just do one thing for me, can't you? Would you do one thing?"

"What?" I am so furious that the frustration of not being able to say what I feel is exhausting. If this man were anyone else, if he were not someone my mother respected, I would tell him to stick one thing up his ass.

"Think of something you really want and then ask for it in Yeshua's name. Anything you want. Don't be afraid to ask for something big. But before you go to bed tonight, just ask for it in Jesus' name. Will you do that for me?"

I roll my eyes. "Yes. I'll do it."

"You *promise*?"

"Yes, I promise. Good night."

"Good night and God bless you, *bubbeleh*!"

Bubbeleh! Who talks like that? Not my relatives. Why do these Messianic Jews have to play up their Jewishness like they're trying out for a Woody Allen film?

I am so angry that I need a while to calm down. Tommy Roe's music is too lively for this mood; I pull out the *It's Now Winter's Day* cassette and replace it with one of Judee Sill's first albums. That's better, except she is singing about "crayon angels" and "waiting for God." At least her God is worth waiting for, not an ogre who condemns people to hell because they did the best they could with the faith they had. Her voice provides a gentle soundtrack as I resume my position on the mattress with Andersen's fairy tales.

Thirteen minutes later. Finally tired enough to go to bed. I rest the book beside me.

Unfortunately I can't turn in until I think of something to pray for in Jesus' name. Selman seems to envision this as some sort of magical scenario where I'll have an impossible prayer answered and then I'll just *have* to believe. But I promised, so I have to do it.

What to ask? I would like to wake up being able to fly. I would like to wake up thirty pounds thinner. I would like to wake up without lazy eye. But it wouldn't be fair to ask God for any of those things because he hasn't done things like that since biblical times—and maybe never, where the instant weight-loss prayer is concerned. So what can I ask God for that he could reasonably answer without too much effort on his part?

I know what. It's something that, at this moment of my life, I want more than anything else in the world—at least, more than anything apart from having a boyfriend who loves me. I want to find Sandy Salisbury.

The past fourteen months have seen me spend hours upon hours and days upon days trying to find and interview everyone who knew Curt Boettcher. With financial support from both Mom and Dad, who were glad to see me engaged in a project that could help me launch a career as a rock historian, I have racked up hundreds of dollars in phone bills interviewing Curt's family, friends, and collaborators. I have also traveled for my Boettcher research, including to Los Angeles, where I visited Valley Center Studios and listened as Curt's former co-workers transferred his collection of reel-to-reels onto digital audio tape. What I heard there—amazing unreleased recordings from the 1960s and '70s—left me more convinced than ever that the world needed to discover Boettcher's genius.

Curt's greatest achievement is the Millennium's *Begin*, so what I most need is to find people who can tell me the story of that album. Thus far, I have interviewed Gary Usher, who was *Begin*'s executive producer; Keith Olsen, who co-produced the album with Curt; and Millennium members Ron Edgar and Doug Rhodes. But given that there were seven men in the Millennium, there may be as many as four surviving members left to find.

Among those four, I am told that one member would likely have the best memory of them all, as he stayed away from drugs and never drank anything stronger than milk. He is moreover a fine pop songwriter with a voice as sunny as his home state of Hawaii. He is Sandy Salisbury, and I don't just want to find him; I have to.

It's not like I haven't tried. I have called Information in area codes throughout California, the last place I know Sandy lived, as well as Hawaii. Then there were the hours I spent in NYU's Bobst library looking through the telephone directories they have stored on sheets of microfiche film, each the size of a large index card.

The painstaking task required taking the microfiche sheets one by one out of their file box, handling them by their edges, and examining them through the reader machine so that they might reveal their microscopic secrets. But a search of the directories of several major cities yielded nothing for Sandy, not even under his real name of Henry G. Salisbury. A wasted afternoon.

Thinking back to that day at Bobst makes me sad for another reason. It was there that I made the crushing discovery that Curt Boettcher's name had indeed been in the LA phone book. If I had rung him up when I first thought of it, I might have reached him before he went into the hospital.

What if Sandy is dying, too? That's not likely; he would only be in his mid-forties. But after what happened with Curt, if I had to endure the tragedy of another near-miss— discovering an idol had died just before I could reach him— it would be the death of *me*.

With that thought, I get up off my mattress and pull the switch on the wall to turn off the overhead light. No need to set the alarm; tomorrow is Friday, so there's no class. I get under the covers and pray:

Dear God, please let me find Sandy Salisbury.

That's not enough. I have to promise God something in return. And of course, to keep my word to Selman, I have to wrap things up by invoking Jesus somehow.

But what can I promise? That I'll believe in Jesus? I couldn't make that promise unless I was sure I could keep it, and I'm not sure. If I did promise, and then tried to believe but couldn't keep it up, wouldn't that be worse than never promising at all? And if I'm on God's bad side now—and surely I must be, since he doesn't stop my suffering—what would it be like if I were a traitor to him?

Dear God, if you let me find Sandy Salisbury, I will go to Beth Israel with Mom this Friday. And I will try to believe. Sorry I can't promise more than that. I will do my best. I ask this in Jesus' name. Amen.

Friday, February 17, 1989, 8:04 a.m. He's in Portland, Oregon.

I wake up with the thought already in my head. I just know, as surely as I know that my mother is in Morristown, New Jersey, and my father is in Washington, D.C., that Sandy Salisbury is in Portland.

My right foot seems to barely skim my dorm room's thin wall-to-wall carpet, and I practically glide the four additional steps it takes to reach the black push-button Trimline telephone on my desk. It feels so strange to float like this; normally I am a klutz.

"Information, what city?"

"Portland. Last name Salisbury. The first name would be either Sandy or Henry."

"I have a Henry Salisbury Real Estate Management on Fifteenth Avenue."

"Yes, I'll take that." Breathlessly I find a piece of scrap paper on my desk and scrawl down the number.

Real-estate management! Of all the conventional day jobs to have! Could it really be Sandy? Was he as straight as all that?

It's only a few minutes after five a.m. in Portland. But it's a business number, so it's unlikely I'll disturb anyone. Probably an answering machine will pick up.

The phone on the other end is ringing. I hold my breath until the familiar click of an answering machine kicks in.

"Hi, this is Sandy . . ."

Tuesday, February 21, 1989, 9:41 p.m. Well, I did it. I did everything I had promised God I would do. I went to Beth Israel last Friday night. I withstood the unwanted hugs and the songs with the repetitive lyrics that drone on and on.

I put my heart into it too, trying to go with the flow, to ride on the wave of love and kindness and goodness and faith that surrounded me at the worship center. I tried to believe that God loved me, that Jesus was real and present somehow in all those faithful people, and that he would make himself present in me as well.

After all, something truly miraculous had happened to me. Sandy called me back after getting my answering-machine message and he was all I had hoped he would be—healthy and happy, with a terrific memory and a heart as warm as the Honolulu sunshine. Wasn't that a sign that God wanted me to believe, that he wanted me to be happy?

On Friday night, faith was a feeling that was in the air. I breathed it in. It remained for a few days like the fading scent of a perfume from a passer-by.

Tonight it is officially gone. I am trying to work up the thoughts that would bring it back. But I can't. And now I am wondering if it was ever really there.

5 I Go to
Pieces

Saturday, May 13, 1989, 5:55 p.m. I am in my room at the Holiday Inn in Fairfax, Virginia, putting on makeup and thinking of the dream I had about Del Shannon a few months back. He was onstage playing his upbeat hit "Hats Off to Larry," only the tempo was slowed to the point where it sounded like a funeral dirge. It sounded haunting and oddly beautiful. When played at half-speed, the augmented chord in the chorus took on an aura of longing.

The next time I spoke with Gary on the phone, I shared my dream with him and he found it amusing. A package arrived from him the following week with a homemade compilation cassette. The track listing on the cassette's cover, meticulously lettered as usual in Gary's print-quality handwriting, included the words, "DEL DIRGE!"

Knowing Gary's skill for locating rare recordings, I was excited. Could it be that he found a real-life instance of the musical arrangement I had heard in my dream? No such luck; it was just Shannon's slowed-down version of the Zombies' "Tell Her No." But it did indeed sound funereal.

The thought of death is in the back of my mind right now as I think about Del and the interview I have lined up with him tonight for *Goldmine*.

For one thing, I have this irrational fear that Del is going to die. I know it's ridiculous. The man is barely fifty years old—at least, if the birth year listed in Joel Whitburn's *Top Pop Singles* is correct—and he seems to be in great shape. He must do at least a hundred tour dates each year. But ever since the soul-crushing experience of discovering I was too late to interview Curt Boettcher, I've been possessed by the fear that every other musician I love is likewise going to die before I can get to him.

Last year, Del's music crept up on me. I had always liked his hits, especially the way he used the plaintive key of A minor to express feelings of loneliness and isolation. Back in the early Sixties, he almost singlehandedly created a genre of moody, mysterious rock songs. Even the Beatles copied him; John Lennon's "I'll Be Back" was an attempt to rework "Runaway."

Still, it wasn't until I saw Del perform live that February that I realized just how special he was. He was headlining one of Richard Nader's Doo-Wop Spectaculars at the Beacon Theatre. But when he took the stage, it was obvious that, despite still being in full possession of his trademark falsetto, he wasn't doo-wop. He played electric guitar, he sang songs he wrote himself, and he rocked. What's more, he didn't rock like an old person trying to act young. I felt like I was watching an alternative-rocker at a downtown watering hole, not a museum piece at an uptown concert hall.

It was then that I knew for certain Del wasn't merely someone who kept rock alive at a time in the early Sixties when lukewarm singers named Bobby dominated hit radio. He was a true artist, and the world needed to know his greatness beyond his handful of hits. Once I realized that, I knew I had to interview him while he was still with the living. Never again do I want a repeat of what happened with Curt Boettcher.

So, part of what I am thinking about now is how glad I am to have a chance to get Del's story before he dies. But I am also thinking about my own death—or, rather, trying not to think about it, at least for one night. It is about as difficult as trying not to think of a purple cow.

This coming Thursday, if all goes well, I will graduate NYU. Mom and Dad will be there—the first time since my bat mitzvah that they'll be in the same place—along with my sister and stepmother. Gary is strongly hinting he may attend too along with his musical partner Dave Rave, who is also a dear friend of mine. So all the people who are closest to me are coming together to show their support as I begin this new stage of my life.

Except that it doesn't feel like a new stage of my life. It feels like the beginning of the end.

College for me has never been about what goes on in the classroom. Most of that has been boring and irrelevant. It's been about having a place in Greenwich Village to live while gaining as much experience as possible in the music business.

Although NYU only permitted me one year of internship credits, I have spent hundreds more hours in assorted internships for no credit, just to get inside an independent record label, a music-publicity firm, or a rock-historian's archive. And that was in addition to writing for national music magazines, booking concerts at Tramps nightclub even though I was too young to drink there, and managing the DJ schedule at CBGB Record Canteen.

During the past four years, I've endured many lonely hours waiting for Gary or another love interest to call; yet, in my music-biz activities, there has never been a dull moment. Always I had an artist to interview, an industry party to attend, or a demo tape to audit for a possible nightclub booking.

Now that is all going to end. None of the places where I interned have positions available. A couple of former supervisors say they might have some freelance work, but the pay would be minimal. And the amount I make from my only writing outlet that pays, *Goldmine*, won't even begin to cover the rent of the shoebox-sized Upper West Side illegal sublet that will soon be my new home.

So I am about to enter the working world at age twenty with . . . what? A degree from NYU, a résumé filled with internships each lasting three to six months, and a portfolio of articles from rock magazines.

When I was in college, I imagined that such a wide variety of experience would set me up for my dream job. But now that I am about to graduate, I fear that employers will take one look at my résumé and toss it into the wastebasket. Meanwhile, my peers, who didn't care about gaining a variety of experience and were willing to bear with boredom, worked their way up the ladder at the first and only place where they interned. They'll graduate into full-time positions in their chosen field; I'll be lucky to get the job I applied for at the reservation desk of Caroline's Comedy Club.

But even if I eventually get the kind of job I really want, will it make me happy?

I thought I would be happy writing Curt Boettcher's biography. But now I find that I only enjoy the research, not the actual writing. In fact, I haven't yet managed to do *any* writing on Curt, and I haven't transcribed a single one of the dozens of interviews I've conducted on him. My depression is so bad that the most I can write is a magazine article; the task of writing a book is too monumental even to begin.

I thought I would be happy with a boyfriend; in fact, I thought I would find my husband while in college, just as Mom found hers—not that *that* worked out. But all I have is Gary, and he refuses to commit.

And I thought I would be happy when I graduated college. That was the last horizon. Now graduation is almost here—and if it doesn't make me happy, there is nothing left.

I am scared. I am scared that when I graduate, I will fall into an emotional black hole. All the hopes I have been using to prop myself up will vanish. I will collapse and there will be no bottom. It will be like those times during the past few years when I could no longer contain my loneliness and my frustration with all the things I hate about myself— being fat, being clumsy, being socially awkward, being an underachiever, not being able to attract a man I love who would love me. Then I will take out the sharpest object that I can find and will try to draw blood, just as I have tried during those times when everything I was trying to suppress bubbled up to the surface. But, unlike in the past, I won't be doing it just for the sake of feeling physical pain to match the pain I have inside. I will be doing it because I actually want to bleed out. And this time—unlike in the past, when I've stopped short of breaking my skin—I may be successful.

But for now I can look forward to interviewing Del backstage tonight before he performs his headlining set at yet another oldies show.

About five and a half hours later. I've lost track of time and don't want to look at the clock because that would be rude. But it must be late, and I can't get over how terrifically gracious Del is in continuing to answer my questions.

From the moment I met Del backstage, he treated me with great kindness and respect. He spoke like he sang, with a Midwestern drawl. There was a softness and warmth to his demeanor that immediately made me feel at ease.

We began the interview there in his dressing room as he awaited his turn to perform. But by the time he was to take the stage, more than half an hour later, I had only managed to ask him about his career up to 1967.

I dashed out to catch Del's performance—every bit as life-affirming as the one I saw him give last year—and then returned backstage. Del was standing with a towel draped around his neck, chatting with a member of one of the opening acts, the Contours. When he saw me, he broke off the conversation and offered to continue the interview at his motel room, since he was staying at the same place as me. What a relief! It would have been terrible to have to return to New York with an incomplete interview, especially since Del was sharing so openly about his life and music, telling stories I had not heard anywhere else.

An hour later, I walked from my motel room to Del's, where I am now. It is just down the walkway from mine on the second floor, overlooking the parking lot.

I was nervous inside at the thought of seeing Del alone in his room. Although I am in awe of him and kind of in love on a spiritual level, he is my dad's age. Also, he is a newly-wed. In fact, after I entered the room, he phoned his bride and offered me the receiver so I could say hello.

Thankfully, he is treating me with the same respect as he did backstage. The only awkward thing is that he is wearing a dressing gown. But there is nothing flirtatious in his manner; it is as though we are old friends.

I am almost at the end of my list of questions. Del is talking about "Walk Away," the song he wrote with Tom Petty and Jeff Lynne that just came out as a single in Australia. He says that, in addition to that recording, he has a number of new songs that he has just recorded in sessions produced by Petty's guitarist, Mike Campbell. There is a chance that the BMG label may put out the recordings; they are holding a meeting in London next week to decide whether to move forward with the release.

That sounds wonderful to me: "I'll say a few prayers that they pick up that record, because . . . "

Del's expression suddenly changes; he looks worried. He interrupts me: "Oh, you don't want to do that, see?"

"Oh, right! You're right!" Why am I saying that? Just to placate him, I guess. I don't actually see why I shouldn't pray for him, but I don't want him to worry.

"No, I think it's dangerous," Del goes on. "I think it's dangerous for me—you don't have to pray for me."

"I'm sorry."

"You can pray for His will for me. That would be great."

"Oh, I will! I will do that!"

"'Cause what if we got the record deal, I get in an airplane, and it goes 'crash'?" Del smiles as he says this and throws up his hands. "Forget it! Hit record with a crash!"

I laugh nervously, embarrassed at my theological faux pas. "You're right, you're right. I'll pray God's will for you."

"God's will for me! That's great!"

"I will! Is it true that George Harrison plays guitar on 'Walk Away'?"

About half an hour later. Del is looking out from the doorway of his room as I walk away. When I gave him a quick upper-body goodbye hug just now—wanting so much to hold him longer but resisting for fear of seeming forward—he said he would watch to make sure I reached my room safely.

As I traverse the hundred feet or so down the outdoor walkway, I try to numb my feelings. The other rooms' windows are dark; my path is lit partly by the moon but mostly by a few dull ceiling bulbs with a pair of moths buzzing around. I reach my room and put the key in the door; Del and I exchange waves and I am alone in my own world again.

As I check to make sure the curtains are closed—having a room entrance facing the outside makes me feel unsafe—I think about what an extraordinary man Del is. What a heart he has! I was young enough to be his daughter and he shared with me as though I were a peer. I came to him as an adoring fan and he treated me as an old friend.

I don't want this evening to end. Preparing for bed, I am only half aware of what I am doing as I remove my makeup and brush my teeth. I want to relive the moments after I hit the stop button on my cassette recorder, when Del pulled out his Sony Walkman and invited me to listen to his latest songwriting demos.

The recordings were sparse and intimate—just voice and guitar—and their lyrics were poignant, as though Del's heart were stripped bare. My favorite was the bittersweet "When I Had You"; its melody is still running through my head.

Before I left, I told Del apologetically that it might take me a while to write up the interview, as I was about to graduate college and needed to find a job. And then I found myself opening up about my depression and my fears for the future.

He was so kind. He said that anytime I needed someone to talk to, I could call him. And he even offered to give me a job reference. It was all so beautiful. I want to cry.

Why can't I find a boyfriend like Del—someone deep, sensitive, and caring, yet also mysterious and creative? Even if Gary finally made the move to New York City from Canada, as he often says he wants to do, even if he finally committed to me, could he ever be as great of heart as this man? And why couldn't I have met Del before he met his wife?

I have to stay alive. Del wants me to. But I want to die.

Sunday, May 14, 1989, 2:03 a.m. The phone next to my bed rings so loudly, it practically gives me a heart attack. Where am I? Oh, yes, still at the Holiday Inn. But who could be calling at this hour? Could it be Del? Does he want me to come back to his room? Is he in love with me after all? What should I say? Of course I'll come back, even though it's wrong.

"Hello?"

The voice on the other end is so grating and is shouting so loud that I practically have a second heart attack. He says he is from the Contours. It must be the guy I saw in the dressing room when I went back to see Del after the concert. He sounds like he is on cocaine.

I exclaim the first thing that comes to mind: "I'm sleeping!"

He keeps shouting, saying I have to see him. He must think I am some kind of a whore. I am so stunned that it takes me a moment to realize I don't have to take this.

"It's two a.m.," I say, trying to sound like I am merely angry and not terrified. "Goodbye!"

My heart is racing so much that it takes me some time to calm down and let sleep return. I feel sick and violated . . .

The sound of voices calling to each other outside wakes me up. My eyes are still closed but I can tell that the morning light is leaking in through the curtains. I remember that

I asked Del last night when he would need to be up, and he said a bus would come for him and the other performers at seven-thirty. Finally I turn to look at the alarm clock: seven-twenty-one.

He's leaving! If I jump out of bed and quickly pull on my dress from last night, I can run out to say one last goodbye to Del and get one last hug.

No. I am staying where I am. For one thing, I can hear the grating voice of the scary Contours guy and I am afraid he might confront me. But more than that, last night with Del was perfect. We were together as friends. Love was there, unspoken, but neither of us did anything we might regret. So I can't go chasing after Del. Doing so would only embarrass myself and mess up a beautiful memory, one I will carry with me for the rest of my life.

My life . . .

As the voices outside grow more distant, another overpowering thought takes hold.

I know that I will never, ever see Del again.

There is no logical reason why I should imagine that, but now I can't get it out of my head. And the idea of it makes me want to die.

Friday, February 9, 1990, 7:19 a.m. Here I am in my closet of an apartment, drying myself off after having to shower in the shared bathroom down the hall. This is what $362.50 a month buys on the Upper West Side.

And for what? Why do I bother getting up at this unearthly hour to take the B train to the D train to the end of the F line, to a gypsy van, just to reach a drab warehouse in Queens?

When I interviewed for my administrative-assistant job at Relativity Records, I thought of the label as an American outlet for British alternative rock, which is what it used to be. Unfortunately, since I arrived in December, they've only been putting out albums by one heavy-metal hair band after another.

Add the fact that my boss is a cokehead who goes out of his way to tell me he doesn't like women, and this job, which was supposed to be my stepping stone to my dream job of signing artists to a major label, is nothing but a dead end. Make that a low-paying dead end, and, worse, one that keeps me from doing the only type of work I enjoy: writing. It's hard to find the time or energy to write when I'm working eight hours a day with a three-hour round-trip commute. Plus I haven't felt like doing much of anything since Gary broke up with me last September.

I turn on the radio, already set to oldies station WCBS-FM, and the tail end of "Runaway" pops out of the speakers. Now I feel worse. Nine months have passed since Del gave me his time, and all I have to show for it is a few pages on a legal pad where I started to transcribe my interview with him before I became distracted by life.

WCBS "Morning Mayor" Harry Harrison speaks over the song's fade. He makes me feel better about waking up when he delivers his daily reminder that "every brand-new day should be unwrapped like a precious gift."

But something is different today. Harry is giving biographical information about Del, but he is not employing his happy voice. It's his concerned voice: "Del Shannon, born Charles Westover, December 30, 1939, in Grand Rapids, Michigan . . ."

I freeze. No. No.

". . . found dead late last night at his home in Santa Clarita, California, apparently from a self-inflicted gunshot wound to the head."

I scream.

My neighbor Carol from down the hall comes rushing in, wearing a bathrobe. "Is everything okay?"

"I'm fine, I'm fine. Sorry for screaming. I just—I just heard on the radio that Del Shannon died. He was a friend of mine."

"I thought *you* had died. Glad you're okay. Sorry about your friend."

She turns around and heads back into her apartment. For a moment I remain standing in place, out of breath. I can't move. I can't think. I don't want to think.

Three hours later. Thank God my boss is out today, because there's no way I can get any work done. I called Jeff at *Goldmine* to let him know I would get my Del interview in to him as soon as possible. He had already heard the news. Then I phoned Del's widow, LeAnne. It was kind of crazy to call her just hours after she found her husband's body, but I felt so helpless and wanted to do something to encourage her.

She picked up the phone right away. I told her how sorry I was, that I would be completing my article on Del soon, and that I was so grateful to have had one of his last interviews.

Her response came between sobs. "He said . . . it was a special interview."

If my heart wasn't broken already, it was then. Here this woman has just found her husband's body, and it's she who's offering me a consoling word.

Just a moment ago I said goodbye to LeAnne and now the thought arises that I need to phone someone else. I need to call Max Crook.

Max is the keyboard genius who played the solos on Del's early smashes "Runaway" and "Hats Off to Larry" using a Musitron—a kind of prehistoric synthesizer that he invented. He remained good friends with Del and will be distressed

to learn that he has died. It would be better if he learned the
news from me than from some reporter who tracked him
down to press him for a comment. Also, since Del moved
recently, Max might not have LeAnne's number. I could do
them both a service by putting them back in touch.

There's just one problem—make that two. I don't have
Max's number and I don't know where he lives.

Del probably told me Max's whereabouts when we spoke,
but my cassette of the interview is at home. I must think.
Where did he say Max was?

New Mexico. That sounds right. But where in New
Mexico? Even though it's all a single area code, the information operator will want me to name a city. Albuquerque
doesn't sound right, and Las Cruces doesn't either. Max lives
in a smaller place.

I press 9 for an outside line and then 1-303-555-1212. As
with the call to LeAnne, it's on Relativity's dime, but I don't
care; this is a mission of mercy. I give the operator Max's
name and say the first town that pops into my mind: "Four
Corners." Is that even a town?

Success! The operator gives me the number. I can't believe I'm actually doing this.

"Hi, Max, my name's Dawn Eden. You don't know me,
but I knew Del Shannon, and I interviewed him. He told
me where you lived. I felt I should call you today because
there is some very sad news . . ."

It's just as I suspected; Max had not heard. It feels so
strange to be the first person to tell him. I offer him Le-
Anne's number and he says yes, he does need it; all my in-
stincts were correct.

As crushed as I am, it is comforting to think that I was
able to do something kind for Max and LeAnne. I feel as
though Del wanted me to help them.

The next thing to do is quit my job. This company is a dark place. I'm not gaining anything by trekking out here to answer phones for a boss who doesn't respect me. What I need is to take a leap of faith, to get back to writing—starting with my article on Del—and trust that I will find a way to make a living doing what I love, even if it takes me a while.

I have to do it. Del would want it that way.

Tuesday, February 13, 1990, 4:34 p.m. I am finally back to transcribing my interview with Del and am at the point where I asked him where Max Crook lived.

"He lives out in the middle of the desert, and he's very religious, and he does his little studio—twenty miles from a town, in the middle of the desert, him and his wife."

No mention of New Mexico—yet I *knew* that was where Max was.

Thursday, May 31, 1990, 2:31 p.m. At last, a fifteen-minute break. There is nothing more boring than waiting for my name to come up at jury duty. It's crazy—the government has required me to come in every day this week just to sit for seven hours in a room with 200 other potential jurors and not get called. To add insult to injury, the pay is only $15 per day, which is what I would make in an hour and a half if I were doing my usual work as a Warner Communications in-house temp.

I head back to the courthouse's pay telephones—a long row of old-fashioned wooden booths, each with a small built-in seat. Choosing the booth farthest away from one that's occupied, I drop a quarter in and phone my answering machine. If it rings more than twice, that means I have no messages, in which case I can hang up and get my quarter back. But it picks up on the second ring, so I punch in my two-digit access code.

It's Domenic Priore. "Hi, Dawn, I have some bad news. I just heard that Gary Usher died . . ."

Gary Usher *dead?* He can't have been much older than fifty. And he was fine when I interviewed him two years ago about his work with Curt Boettcher. How can all these people I admire die on me? I feel like I am stuck in a bad movie.

Forty-three minutes later. Finally! After four days of sitting around, the court let me go and told me I don't have to return. I head back to the phone booths; it's early enough that I may still be able to catch Doug Wygal.

Doug and I met a few years back when he played drums for one of my favorite local bands, Deep Six. He has an amazing job producing reissues for CBS Special Products, part of the Columbia label, which happens to own the two greatest recordings of Curt Boettcher's career: the Sagittarius album *Present Tense*, which Curt co-produced with Gary Usher, and the Millennium album *Begin*.

Somehow Doug heard about my research, and last year he suggested I might compile a Curt Boettcher memorial album for him. But he was vague about when it might happen, and I didn't press him because the possibility seemed like such a long shot. Given that Columbia had yet to put many of its best-selling Sixties albums out on CD, it didn't seem likely that they would rush to reissue something so obscure as *Begin*.

But now that Usher has died, perhaps there is an audience for an album that would honor both him and Boettcher. Usher is far better known than Curt; his name is on dozens of hit records, including classics by the Beach Boys and the Byrds.

So I dig out another quarter and call. Doug answers; we exchange greetings and I tell him Usher has died. The news doesn't affect him like it affected me—he never knew the man—but he is sorry for my sake.

When I bring up the possibility of a memorial album, Doug suggests we discuss it in his office. It's hard to tell whether he is seriously interested or just being polite. I offer to come in tomorrow, but he says he has meetings; Monday morning should be good if I call first.

I say goodbye and emerge from the booth, my emotions swirling in all directions—grief from the shock of Usher's death, fear at the prospect that other artists I love might die, excitement at the thought that my hopes for a CD of Boettcher's music might finally come to pass, guilt at the thought that I am self-centered in finding joy at a time like this.

The sun is bright and the traffic is loud as I emerge outside to make my way to the Chambers Street station to catch the subway back uptown.

I so want to call Gary right now—the other Gary, my now ex-boyfriend. He loves Usher's music and he would understand how I feel. What's more, he knows much better than me how record labels work, so he could advise me on what to say when I meet with Doug.

But I can't do it. Since he left me, I've called a few times to tell him some piece of news that only he would appreciate. Each time, he was courteous, but the distance in his voice chilled me. After hanging up, I felt bereft. He loves someone else and he will never love me.

At least there's my neighbor Michael Mazzarella. Dear Michael! I would so love to be his girlfriend, but he only likes me as a friend. Yet, unlike nearly every other man I've wanted who didn't want me back, he is really serious about friendship; it's not just an empty word to him. So he hasn't hurt me like others have.

Michael knows the record business. He's even worked as a personal assistant to Atlantic label founder Ahmet Ertegun. I'll tell him about my conversation with Doug and he'll know what to do.

About four hours later. I write in my journal:

Michael Mazzarella just talked w/me & I told him of Doug Wygal's interest in Boettcher/Usher memorial album. He was very pessimistic. I tried to persuade him that it was worth it for me to keep my hopes up. A few minutes later, as I was going back into my apt., he said to me, "I just had a feeling—that record is going to come out." He had what Mom would call a vision, discernment. I think it came from God.

6 Did You Ever Have to Make Up Your Mind?

Thursday, October 5, 1995, 8:46 p.m. For once, I am thankful to be unable to drive. The pope is in New York and traffic is insane.

Earlier tonight, while I was in my apartment in Hoboken, New Jersey, getting ready to leave for the city, the traffic reporter on WCBS-FM was issuing warnings every ten minutes about "papal gridlock." Apparently the man from Rome had the Lincoln Tunnel all to himself as he headed across the river to do his thing tonight at Giants Stadium, which is only about five miles from where I live.

But it didn't matter to me because all I had to do to enter Manhattan was take the underground PATH train to Ninth Street and Sixth Avenue and walk to my favorite Village restaurant, Quantum Leap on West Third Street, for a late dinner. Now, having devoured my usual Mexican Fiesta

Platter, I am fortified to walk to the Mercury Lounge on Houston Street for the Robyn Hitchcock concert I am reviewing for Sonicnet.

The walk will take about twenty minutes, giving me time to think. I don't really want to be alone with my thoughts, but I don't have much of a choice, since I'm not one of those people who can cross city streets while listening to a Walkman—too dangerous.

When I was walking to Quantum Leap, the skies looked threatening; now it is drizzling. Walking in this weather becomes a kind of *pas de deux* as I try to counter the wind as it persistently tries to invert my umbrella.

I should be happy. I am closer than ever to doing what I want to do and living the kind of life I want to live.

So why do I still have to convince myself every day that life is worth living?

Every time I try to trace what went wrong, I keep coming back to my decision to major in music business instead of journalism.

My intentions were noble. The music-business degree would prepare me to work at a major label. There I could improve the artistic quality of pop music by signing artists who were better than most of those who were then on the radio.

And I really did have a knack for discovering performers who deserved a wider audience. Artists I followed before they were signed, such as the Smithereens and They Might Be Giants, have achieved major-label success. The singer of the Long Island band I booked to play my high school, the Mosquitos, went on to write a hit for the reunited Monkees.

But upon graduating NYU, I was forced to come to terms with the extent to which the music world had changed during a few short years. There was less and less room on the radio for the Sixties-inspired pop music that I loved. Moreover, my ears had grown sensitive to the point where I couldn't abide music made with the all-digital recording process that commercial-radio programmers had come to expect. What passed for a "modern" sound struck me as cold. Since it was increasingly unlikely that a major-label job would enable me to promote music I actually liked, there was little point in sticking with my original career plan.

At the same time, I was discovering that something I had been doing throughout my college years as a hobby—researching and writing about the oldies artists I loved—was in fact a marketable talent.

The pivotal moment came in the summer of 1990 when Doug Wygal at CBS Special Products decided that, instead of putting out a Curt Boettcher/Gary Usher memorial album, he would reissue the Millennium album *Begin*. He hired me to write the liner notes for the release, which led to my writing a feature article on Boettcher and Usher for *Goldmine*, which led to—well, I wish it had led to my writing a biography of Curt. That never happened. I tried to find a publisher and couldn't, and I wasn't about to write it without knowing if it would reach readers.

But I did become known as the world's foremost expert on Curt Boettcher, for what it's worth. Better still, Doug gave me more liner-note assignments and I started to become better known as a rock historian. Then I had the great fortune to meet Ron Furmanek just when he was looking for someone to write liner notes for loads of reissues that he was putting together for EMI, including CDs by Jan & Dean, Eddie Cochran, Irma Thomas, and the Hollies. Already I was one of the youngest working rock historians; with Ron's support, I became the most prolific female liner-note writer in rock history. Not that I had much competition—the others could be counted on one hand.

I wish I were getting so many assignments now. Unfortunately, now that so many classic records have come out on CD, labels are trimming their reissue programs. Then there are the labels that try to save money by hiring superfans to write their liner notes, people who don't care about getting paid so long as they can get their name onto their favorite artist's CD.

Still, this year so far hasn't been a complete washout. Four different labels have put out CDs with my liner notes, with one assignment coming all the way from Germany.

And things are looking up. My friend Bill Pitzonka, who knows bubblegum music like I know Curt Boettcher, says the Varese Vintage label is considering hiring us as a team to assemble a series of compilations, to be called *Sunshine Days*, to cash in on the current underground interest in West Coast-style soft pop of the 1960s. It would necessarily include million-selling singles like Spanky & Our Gang's "Sunday Will Never Be the Same" and the Critters' "Mr. Dieingly Sad," but I hope the label won't limit our choices to the biggest hits. Now that the musical genre I've been writing about for a decade is finally hip, I'd like to help listeners discover great soft-pop records that haven't yet been digitized.

Plus, RCA finally released the Harry Nilsson anthology *Personal Best* after delaying it nearly a year in the wake of the singer's untimely death. I was so fortunate to land that assignment; the collection earned rave reviews in just about every major publication, even supermarket magazines like *People*. And I'm still amazed that I was able to do the last interview with Nilsson, just eight days before he died.

Too bad the head of reissues at RCA won't hire me now, since I disobeyed his order not to let Nilsson see the list of songs that the label was planning to put on his own best-of. But what the heck was I supposed to do? There was the artist himself right in front of me, in his living room, telling me that he was so ill that he could die at any moment. Four-fifths of his heart was already dead, he said, and he had diabetic neuropathy that affected his feeling in his fingers. And my boss wanted me to elicit quotes from him on dozens of songs, yet I couldn't show him the very list of songs that RCA was going to present as the greatest works of his career?

Really, RCA should thank me. If I hadn't shown Nilsson that list when I did, he would never have had any input on the track selection for the collection. The label wouldn't even have been able to call it *Personal Best*.

Well, at least the Nilsson assignments and all my other liner notes helped me get my name in front of editors. Now I have more journalistic outlets than ever. I'm getting regular assignments from the British magazine *Mojo*, the hip downtown weekly *New York Press*, and Sonicnet, which is not actually a print magazine but a site on the World Wide Web. Plus I'm getting part-time work from a Hoboken weekly, which is not so glamorous as rock journalism but it's still writing. And that's not even counting my unpaid work interviewing rock bands on Manhattan Public Access TV's "Videowave" and appearing as a music expert on the FX Network's "Sound FX." My public profile is so high that people are actually starting to recognize me on the street.

For the first time in two years, I am so successful that I have not had to ask Mom or Dad for money for literally months. Dad did give me a nice check for my birthday, but I didn't ask him; he just sent it because he wanted to. I should be happy.

But there's that journalism degree I never got. That's hurting me now. Getting steady freelance work is really hard; there's no guarantee I can ride out a third month in a row without parental assistance. To move up as a rock writer,

I need a regular job at a place like *Rolling Stone*, *Billboard*, or *Spin*, only I can't break in at any of those places. And the reason I can't break in is because they are looking for journalists with full-time experience. They are not going to hire a twenty-seven-year-old with only freelance gigs on her résumé when they can take their pick of younger writers who have been working steadily in editorial departments since college.

I thought I was so smart, avoiding studying journalism because I already knew how to write. Really, I was dumb. I made a mistake that is going to haunt me for the rest of my professional life, and there is nothing I can do to undo it.

Walking down Great Jones Street by Lafayette Street now. I so want to detour to Tower Books to see if the October *Mojo* has come in, but I'm not going to. It's late enough already and I need to get to the Mercury Lounge.

So I'm not happy because I have hit a dead end in my career. But I wouldn't feel so much like my career had to make me happy, if it weren't for that I don't have a boyfriend. And I don't have a boyfriend because . . .

Because I messed up. Because I didn't let Gary be the first one. That's why.

In my memory, all roads lead back to that failed relationship. It's terrible, but it's true. After six years, it still hurts so much. He's married now, married to the woman he left me for, and it's still a raw wound.

I've been thinking about this, really thinking about it, and I've had a lot of time to think about it. And I'm convinced that Gary left me because I wasn't experienced, and the woman he wanted was, and he didn't want to deal with the burden of being the first one. If only I hadn't been so hung up on waiting for him to say "I love you," none of this would have happened.

It took me some time, but I did finally become experienced. I got so sick of men thinking I was some kind of prude for waiting for an "I love you" that I finally lost my virginity to a man I didn't love, just to get it over with so I might be a viable partner for the right man. My virginity had become an albatross, an embarrassing keepsake of my juvenile dreams. It made me self-conscious and kept me from being able to interact with a potential boyfriend like a normal person.

That was three and a half years ago. Since then I have been searching for another man like Gary. Someone creative and witty, who loves music but also reads books and thinks deep thoughts. But more than that, I want a man who is alive, who has hope, who initiates good things rather than waiting for good things to come to him. Why is it that I am always the encourager in relationships? Why can't I find a man who will encourage *me*?

Most often I meet men in nightclubs; some are attractive, but typically they drink too much or smoke pot, which pretty much kills their initiative. That was another thing about Gary—he didn't smoke, avoided drugs, and almost never drank. Why can't I find someone like that?

Except for a brief relationship last year that fizzled, there has been no one. No one to tell me that I am loved, no one to make me feel needed. So I end up trying just to find a man who will take my mind off my loneliness and make me feel desirable, even if it is only for one night. And I hate myself for it, because the whole pursuit makes me feel superficial and I end up losing friends because I make a fool of myself.

Almost at the Mercury Lounge. Just passed the Mars Bar and now I can see the Katz's Delicatessen sign glowing in the distance.

And here's the craziest part of it all: if I sincerely try to imagine what my life would be like had I married Gary, I can't picture how I could have been happy with him. In fact, if I try to imagine marrying *any* man, I can't picture what marital happiness looks like. And that's scary. I want to be loved more than anything else in the world; I want to be *in* love. But I'm scared that if I got what I wanted, something would still be missing.

It's not that I'm afraid of losing my attraction to my husband. I'm afraid that even the most attractive, most big-hearted, most creative man would never be able to understand me the way I want to be understood.

What if it is simply impossible for me to be happy, whether I am alone or with a husband? What then? How would it be worth it to stay alive?

The Mercury Lounge, and just in time; the rain is pouring down now. Inside the front door, a young man with a ponytail and a beat-up black leather jacket asks me for identification.

"My ID?" I am shocked. The drinking age is twenty-one, but East Village rock clubs almost never card; only tourist traps do. "Wow, it's not every day I get asked for that! I'm twenty-seven."

"Yeah, sorry, but I need to see some ID. Mayor Giuliani's been cracking down . . ."

"Gosh, I'm really sorry, I've never been asked for it here, so I didn't bring it. I'm on the guest list—my name is Dawn Eden and I'm reviewing tonight's show for Sonicnet. Here, I can show you my crow's feet—" I draw near to him and point to my right eye.

The doorman laughs. "It's all right," he says, and waves me back. Beyond him is a young man with dark curly hair and a Sonic Youth t-shirt seated at a small table. He finds my name on the guest list and stamps my hand. Thankfully they use the black-light stamps here, so I won't have to worry about the mark being visible. With the ordinary kind, it sometimes takes days for the ink to come off, even with scrubbing.

Mercury Lounge is set up so that getting to the performance room in the back requires walking around the bar. The bar is where people hang out so they might see and be seen. Unless the opening act is particularly well-known, most record-industry folk remain in the barroom so they can talk until the headline act appears. So I need to keep a careful eye out as I make my way through, in case there is anyone I know or want to know.

The first acquaintance I see is Scott McCaughey. It's been a few years since we've seen each other—the last time was when I caught his band the Young Fresh Fellows in London—but I'd know his frizzed-out mane anywhere.

"Scott!" I exclaim. "It's Dawn Eden!"

"Dawn!" he says with a warm smile. "I've been reading you in *Mojo*!"

"Wow, thank you! It's been a while! What have you been up to?"

"Oh, you know," he says, with a quick glance to his left as though he's looking for someone. "Touring with the band."

"Which band?" I ask as I mentally run through the possibilities. He's been in so many. The Young Fresh Fellows? The Minus 5? The Squirrels?

"R.E.M."

How could I have forgotten? I read that Scott would be filling out R.E.M.'s lineup for their current tour. In fact, aren't they playing the Meadowlands tomorrow? Probably the only reason they're not there tonight is that the sports complex's management didn't want them to play the arena at the same time the pope was doing his thing at the stadium next door.

"Oh, gosh, of course. Sorry. I was thinking of your *own* bands."

A slight young woman with chestnut hair approaches Scott from his left. He introduces her, a bit haltingly, as "Tabitha."

I don't recognize Tabitha, but I gather from Scott's hesitance to introduce her that she is Tabitha Soren, the MTV News reporter. Since moving away from home, I haven't owned a TV—it's too distracting, and I'm already far too distracted. So I read magazines and the *New York Times* to learn who the current pop-culture celebrities are. Soren's name stood out because I recalled her being associated with WNYU Radio when I was in college.

"Didn't you go to NYU?" I ask.

Soren looks stunned by my question. Apparently it's the last thing she was expecting me to say. Probably people normally ask her what it was like to interview Kurt Cobain.

I politely explain how I remembered her, then excuse myself and move on down the bar. She still has a deer-caught-in-headlights expression as I walk away.

Part of me feels a smug satisfaction in acting blasé before Soren's glorious celebrity. The lowly Dawn Eden of "Sound FX" and "Videowave" has just one-upped the great MTV star Tabitha Soren in the coolness wars! Part of me feels guilty, as though I have not been cool but simply cruel. And part of me just feels foolish for caring what Soren or anyone thinks of me.

There is a clean-shaven man in his early forties awaiting a drink at the bar who stands out in his crisp white shirt and polka-dotted bowtie. I take a good look at his face—yes, he surely is Timothy White, editor-in-chief of *Billboard*. Now there's a place I would love to work.

White saw me looking, so I have to introduce myself right away. Think quickly! He wrote a book on the Beach Boys that delved deeply into Los Angeles rock history; maybe he'll know my work in that field.

"Timothy! I don't believe we've ever met, but we have mutual friends. My name is Dawn Eden. I write for *New York Press* and for *Mojo*, and I wrote the liner notes for the Harry Nilsson *Personal Best* collection . . ."

His face softens into a smile; it's muted but genuine. "Didn't you write about Curt Boettcher?"

"Yes, that's right!" I sound a little too giddy, but it's not every day that someone knows me from my Boettcher research. "So glad you know about that!"

We are interrupted for a moment as the bartender brings him his drink. It gives me time to think about something specific to say to compliment him on his work with *Billboard*.

"I want to tell you, I really appreciate how much you've done to open up *Billboard* to indie and alternative artists. Things like your recent feature story on 'space-age bachelor pad music'—*Billboard* never would have paid attention to a trend like that in the old days."

"Thank you, but I really have to give credit to my staff, like Chris Morris, who wrote that article. You haven't written for us, have you?"

"No, I haven't."

"Well, we'll have to do something about that. Tell me, what do you think of the power-pop revival? Have you been following it?"

I am so stunned that for a moment I am tempted to look around to see if there is a hidden camera. White must have seen my work in *New York Press*, where practically every week I rave about a favorite indie power-pop act.

"Oh, yes!" I exclaim. "In fact, I've been following that scene for a while, and I know some of the people at labels like Big Deal and Not Lame."

"We should have you do something on that. Would you be willing to write about the power-pop scene from an industry perspective, looking at what's going on with sales, distribution, radio . . .?"

"Oh, yes!" I must sound like a broken record. "I have many contacts in that scene and I'm sure I could, um, do a, um, a good—a th-—a thorough—"

Gosh, I hate my stammer. It's worse when I'm excited and trying to make a good impression.

Timothy rescues me. "Why don't you give me a call when I'm in the office and I'll put you in touch with our features editor?" He gives me his card.

"Sure! I'll do that! Thanks so much! Nice meeting you!"

I walk away in a kind of daze, which lasts a few more seconds until I reach the band room. There, the opening act, a female Australian trio I've never heard of, is singing a deadly serious folk song about injustice. There is a smattering of applause from the small audience—the bar is far more crowded right now—and then the singer says, "Our next song's the true story of a boy who was taken away from his parents and put in a mental hospital and then in a jail, and then he committed suicide by stabbing himself in the eye with a paintbrush. This song is for him, and the many others like him."

Ick. I head back to the bar for my usual drink of club soda with a splash of Rose's Lime Juice. It's cheaper than booze and better for my brain, especially when I am on an assignment.

About an hour and a half later. Hitchcock is nearing the end of his set. Since I managed to land a spot all the way up by the stage in this now-packed room, I have a good vantage point to admire his appearance. He is as handsome as I remember from that Tower Records performance nine years ago, only with slightly softer features, his bangs sporting a couple of streaks of gray. His singing and playing are as beautiful as I remember too, except that his voice sounds a little scratchier.

Although Hitchcock began the set playing an acoustic guitar that made his melancholy songs sound plangent and almost hopeful, he has switched to a black Fender electric that adds a darker edge. Just now, he strummed the final chord of "You and Oblivion," a drony elegy mixing memories of a romantic parting with intimations of death. With the sound of the reverberating strings still hanging in the air, he reaches down to take a swig from the bottle of Poland Spring water by the set list at his feet.

I join in the applause, which is difficult to do while holding a small spiral notepad and pen. Sonicnet wants me to write the review with timestamps noting what happens when, so I look at my watch and jot down "11:41." How typical of a New York rock club to keep people out so late on a Thursday night. At this rate, I won't make it home until at least one.

Hitchcock adjusts the angle of his microphone. "I'd like to dedicate this one to the pope, but I don't think I'm going to." He pauses as the audience laughs—myself included. "So, I'll dedicate it to the R.E.M. guys instead, because none of us were influenced by Tom Petty."

Translation: he and R.E.M. were emulating the Byrds before Petty took his own Byrds-influenced jangly guitar sound into the pop charts. As if to demonstrate, Hitchcock launches into the arpeggiated riff that begins "Queen of Eyes," a Byrds-inspired song he wrote and recorded thirteen years ago with his band the Soft Boys. I let out an approving cheer.

About forty minutes later. I am tired and really should be heading home, but something makes me stick around.

Once Hitchcock finished his encore, I loitered by the backstage entrance with a copy of the Millennium's *Begin* CD in hand. Given his love of Sixties Los Angeles pop, he might already know the album. And if he didn't know it, he should. I fantasized about how wonderful it would be if he would spread the word about Boettcher's genius.

And maybe, I thought, if Hitchcock were already a fan of the Millennium, he might become a fan of me as well.

But Hitchcock emerged from backstage quickly with a few people around him, one apparently being his girlfriend. When I introduced myself as a Sonicnet reviewer and handed him the Millennium CD, adding a short spiel about Curt Boettcher, he was polite but perfunctory. There was no indication that he knew or particularly cared who Boettcher was.

I'm not crushed. It would have been nice if Hitchcock were more impressed with my gift, but I never really expected that he would take to me. He's always given the impression of being out of reach, and his oblique lyrics only add to the mystery.

Sometimes the more distant a man is, the more I feel I have to make him love me. But I don't feel that way about Hitchcock, for some reason. Right now, having accomplished what I came for, all I feel is an extra bit of emptiness. There is one less thing to hope for and one more reason to feel lonely.

So I should head home. But I can't. There's nothing waiting for me there except a noon deadline.

Most of the crowd has dispersed to the bar or gone home. The only people left now in the band room are me, a bald technician in a black t-shirt who is disassembling cords from the stage equipment, and about fifteen people chatting at tables, apparently all friends or acquaintances of Hitchcock. I strike up a conversation with one of them, a young male musician I know vaguely from the local scene; he points out to me Grant-Lee Phillips and the members of his band Grant Lee Buffalo, who are enjoying a night off from their tour as supporting act to R.E.M.

As I try to make small talk with the musician, not to flirt but just to avoid having to leave, I hear the sound of someone softly fingerpicking an acoustic guitar. Turning toward the source of the sound, I see Hitchcock less than ten feet away; he is sitting, Judy Garland-style, on the edge of the stage, guitar in lap. This must be how he calms down after the adrenaline rush of playing a concert.

I turn back toward my conversation partner and find him chatting with the member of Grant Lee Buffalo seated by him. Fine with me; it leaves me free to keep my eyes on Hitchcock, who is now gently singing one of the few Bob Dylan songs I really like: "It's All Over Now, Baby Blue."

This is unbelievable. Robyn Hitchcock, who just performed the first show of a two-night stand at a downtown New York club that holds hundreds, is now playing gorgeous songs for an audience of fifteen.

I glance back at the people at the tables and they are continuing their conversation as though nothing noteworthy is happening. Perhaps they don't want to make Hitchcock feel self-conscious. But I don't care. If he's performing, I'm listening.

Hitchcock finishes the final chorus of the Dylan tune. His friends pause their conversations to applaud; I join in, restraining my enthusiasm to match the subdued level of their handclaps. Now Robyn is leaning his ear close to his guitar so he might retune a flat A-string.

There is one song I had hoped he would perform tonight that he didn't do. It's a Psychedelic Furs tune that I've heard him play live on the radio. I so want to call out for it, but I don't want to break the mood.

Oh, what have I got to lose except my pride? Whatever happens, nothing will be as embarrassing as the time I offered to be his table.

I moderate my voice so it's only just loud enough for Hitchcock to hear me: "The Ghost in You."

Did he hear me? He is still tuning, now working on his D-string.

He begins rhythmically strumming a single chord. It sounds familiar. Could it be?

His voice is so soft, it is almost a whisper. But I can tell what he is singing. It is my song. Now it is ours.

The Grant Lee Buffalo guys and their girlfriends are still chatting as though nothing is happening. I pull my chair away from the table to better hear Robyn. It feels as though he and I are together in a world where it is just the two of us and this song.

He is on the second verse now.

I know Robyn is not in love with me. He is only being kind. Tonight he will share a bed with his girlfriend.

Yet somehow I feel as though he is giving me something more valuable than if he and I were physically intimate. This moment is actually better than anything I might experience if I made love to him, or to anyone. I don't know how that is. It just is.

I only wish it could go on forever. But the song is almost at its end. Robyn is singing, "Love, love, love is only heaven away."

Saturday, December 16, 1995, 4:13 p.m. "Sorry, hold on just one moment; the microphone just fell off."

I hate it when this happens. Ben Eshbach, songwriter and lead singer/guitarist of the Sugarplastic, is waiting patiently on the other end of the line somewhere in Los Angeles, while I sit on the edge of my futon in Hoboken and fumble with the cheap suction-cup microphone I bought at Radio Shack.

Pressing with all the strength my right thumb can muster, I manage to get the little rubber cup to adhere once more to the back of my black Trimline phone. Then I ask Ben to repeat his last answer.

The Sugarplastic is one of several bands I am interviewing for a feature on power pop I am writing for my latest freelance outlet: *CompuServe WOW*, an online publication that launches in the spring. It was my *Billboard* cover story on the power-pop subculture that caught the attention of *WOW*'s entertainment editor.

When the Sugarplastic's debut album *Radio Jejune* arrived in the mail, I knew it was something special. Not only was it a super-catchy feast of miniaturism—with choruses within choruses and hooks within hooks—but Eshbach's lyrics were dazzlingly intricate, loaded with internal rhymes. He somehow managed to be erudite without being pretentious. Rather, he showed a playfulness that reminded me of Lewis Carroll. One of his songs even borrowed a nonsense exclamation from Carroll's "Jabberwocky"—"Callooh! Callay!"—and made it work as a pop lyric.

With that in mind, I ask Ben what he's been reading lately. His response doesn't ring any bells—it's a book I've never heard of by an author I've never heard of. I make a mental note to read it so I can impress him when the Sugarplastic perform in New York. They're sure to come out here sooner or later, since their next album is coming out on a major label, Geffen Records.

About three hours later. I don't know why Häagen-Dazs lists calories on its label for a four-ounce serving size of chocolate sorbet. Everybody knows that a true serving size is an entire pint. It comes to 520 calories, and I am entitled to them because all I had for dinner was takeout steamed chicken and vegetables from the corner Chinese restaurant's "diet menu." That was only 380 calories; hence 520, plus my thousand-calorie brunch, will still keep me under 1,950 calories for the day.

If I have mastered anything, it is the art of eating a pint of frozen dessert while sitting on my bed and reading. With (1) my back against a firm pillow on the wall—the pillow must be firm to provide the right support—and (2) my knees pulled up with the book resting on them at an angle facing me, I can then (3) hold the pint container in my left hand while at the same time using my hand's weight to hold the pages open. This leaves my right hand free to spoon the dessert into my mouth and, when necessary, rest the spoon in the container so that I may wipe my mouth with a napkin.

It sounds like a lot of trouble just for a pint of Häagen-Dazs, but I am willing to do it because this is how I keep going. I trek into New York City to see a Park Avenue psychiatrist every Tuesday at 1 p.m. at my father's expense and I am on two different prescribed medications to remedy what my psychiatrist diagnoses as "Major Depression." But the medications don't do what they're supposed to do—keep me from thinking about harming myself—so I have to come up with other ways to survive until tomorrow morning.

Since I don't see any point in messing myself up further by abusing alcohol or illegal drugs, since there are no good concerts tonight, and since there is no romantic prospect in my life, the only option left to distract me is junk food. Or, rather, junk food, the Phil Ochs *Greatest Hits* CD I just put on to give my ears a break from power pop, and the book I picked up at Barnes & Noble earlier this evening.

The book—now resting precariously on my knees, in danger of being stained with chocolate sorbet—is the one Ben Eshbach recommended: *The Man Who Was Thursday* by G.K. Chesterton. The copyright page on this Penguin Classics edition says it was first published in 1908. Other than Lewis Carroll and Hans Christian Andersen, I haven't read any authors that old since high school.

I like the way the novel begins. There is a debate between two poets about what constitutes poetry. One of them is straight-laced, calling himself a poet of law and order; the other proudly proclaims he is an anarchist.

It doesn't seem that I'm supposed to like the anarchist. But certainly he seems the more interesting of the two, especially as he argues that poetry is meant to stir things up. "The poet will be discontented even in the streets of heaven," he says. "The poet is always in revolt."

Naturally the poet of law and order doesn't like this. He retorts, "Revolt in the abstract is—revolting. It's mere vomiting."

Well, that got my attention. If nothing else, it's pretty modern language for the Edwardian era.

I read on. Chesterton writes, still in the voice of the law-loving poet: "'It is things going right,' he cried, 'that is poetical!'"

That's interesting. I pause a moment to reflect upon it and realize that I have scraped the very last drop of now-melted sorbet. Now I can put the empty pint container on my night table and stretch out my legs a bit.

I return to the law-and-order poet's speech. "Yes," he says, "the most poetical thing, more poetical than the flowers, more poetical than the stars—the most poetical thing in the world is not being sick."

The passage takes me by surprise. It actually gives me goosebumps.

Again I lift up my eyes from the book, thinking—now I'm not even sure about what—and then bend my neck down to reread the passage. I am not so much rereading it as staring at it for a while.

It's so simple. But it feels *true*. I want to know that poetry.

7 Little Bit O' Soul

Thursday, May 7, 1998, 11:44 a.m. I stand beneath Waterloo Bridge on the South Bank of the Thames, turning my gaze downward to feverishly scan spine after spine and row after row of used hardcovers. Colin wasn't kidding; this is an amazing selection of books for a flea market.

From my left, an arm wearing a button-down tattersall-check shirt thrusts itself into my line of view, holding an old paperback. I reflexively jump back; the sudden intrusion startled me, as my lazy left eye is slow to notice things.

But it's just Colin, my . . . I want to call him my boyfriend, though it feels strange; our relationship is so new and precarious.

"Look," Colin says. "Recognize this one?"

It's a cowboy novel; the cover features a painting of a woman on a rearing horse as a cowboy on another horse grabs her horse's reins.

"Is that one of yours? One of the—the ones you own?"

"I've got the original, framed. It's the first cover Edward Mortlemans painted for Pan Books."

"Wow," I reply, hoping I sound appropriately enthusiastic. If I want Colin to appear interested when I discuss my own passion for underappreciated Sixties 45-rpm records, the least I can do is try to appreciate vintage paperback-cover art. Colin steps back over to the paperback tables.

This is the second full day of my two-week trip to stay with Colin, and our first time out together in London. We met briefly last November when I flew here for the Zombies record-release party; he expressed interest in hiring me as a freelance writer on his rock-encyclopedia project and gave me his card.

Our chemistry began after I returned home, when we started to correspond via email. He flirted; I flirted back, and soon we were chatting on the phone—at his expense, thankfully.

Things sped up when Colin flew into New York City in March for a business meeting. We hadn't been together more than twenty-four hours when he told me he loved me and was seriously thinking he might want me for his next wife. He also bestowed upon me a pet name: Bundle.

There was a lot to like about him. For starters, he was English, handsome in an elfin kind of way, a music lover and collector, and an entrepreneur and homeowner. He was older than me, which was a plus, but not old enough to be my father—another plus. Also, he was a devoted dad to the children of his first ex-wife—or was it his second? I forget. He has three exes all told.

As he opened up about his past, I got the impression he married women first and asked questions later. And I couldn't tell whether his ex-wives left him, or he left them, or both.

Colin could tell I needed time to think about whether I wanted to be wife No. 4. So he offered to fly me over to England for two weeks to see how well I might fit into his life.

And the answer thus far is . . . maybe? There's no question that Colin and I bond well on a physical level. But I don't yet feel relaxed around him.

There is a charming boyishness about him, sometimes even a Peter Pan-like air of abandon. Yet the more time I spend with him, the more I see that he is not really open to new experiences, especially ones that might challenge him. He is settled and satisfied with his home, his daily routine, and his method of operating his business. Although he says he wants me to share his life, I don't have the impression he has any particular interest in sharing *my* life.

Still, I really want it to work. It's not like I enjoy being alone. And there are worse things than living in a beautiful converted barn in Ingatestone, England, with a handsome, wealthy husband who helps me publish my writings. In two and a half months, I will turn thirty. If it's hard to find a decent husband now, it's not going to get any easier in the future.

The sight of a familiar name on a book spine interrupts my reverie: G.K. Chesterton, *The Flying Inn*.

Could this be any good if I've never heard of it? The bookseller has wedged it between other works of similar vintage, one by the limerick writer Hilaire Belloc and another by some lady with the *veddy* British name of Evelyn Waugh. I gingerly extricate it, hoping it won't turn out to be poetry.

A gentle flip through the book's yellowed pages reveals it is a novel. I am relieved and excited.

Ever since reading *The Man Who Was Thursday*, which was so good, I have been trying to track down more works by Chesterton, both fiction and nonfiction. Normally I wouldn't be so excited about an author who has such an obvious Christian agenda. But Chesterton's not like any of the Christians I know, apart from my mother. For one thing, he's witty—on a genius level—and even subversive; for another, he doesn't seem to believe that being a Christian solves all of a person's problems.

So far, my favorite work of his apart from *Thursday* is his novel *The Ball and the Cross*. There are things in it that I don't quite get, such as the references to British historical figures like the Jacobites. But I like how Chesterton keeps pressing the idea that there has to be some meaning to life, otherwise there is no point in living. There's that powerful moment in *Thursday* when he has a character say, "I wish I knew why I was hurt so much."

Colin returns to my side, bearing a small pile of books. I turn to him and smile. "I found a novel by G.K. Chesterton that I didn't even know existed."

"Uh-huh."

"And this," I add, showing him *Forever Ealing: A Celebration of the Great British Film Studio.*

"Oh, that's all right. There's a better book on Ealing by Charles Barr."

He picks up both of my books and adds them to his pile. "We could watch an Ealing film tonight," he muses. "Have you seen *The Lavender Hill Mob?*"

"Actually, that's one of the ones I haven't seen."

Sunday, May 10, 1998, 7:20 a.m. The first sound I hear after shutting off the alarm clock is that beautiful birdsong emanating from outside Colin's bedroom window, the same one I first heard a few days ago. I think Colin said it was a nightingale? Parting the scarlet curtains, I try to locate the song's source, but all I can see is the brilliant–yellow rapeseed field and, in the distance, the ancient tower of the village church.

It was nice of Colin to let me have his bedroom for the rest of my stay even though he stopped sleeping with me. He is probably still asleep in his guest room down the hall.

I look in the mirror above the dresser and my hair is going off in several wrong directions, still damp from last night's shower. A few days ago Colin would have found it sexy.

As I finger through my clothes hanging in Colin's rosewood wardrobe, it's hard to find anything suitable for church. Perhaps I can get away with the electric-orange vintage Hawaiian sundress if I put on my denim jacket over it; at least it hits below the knee.

I am still trying to process what happened Thursday afternoon. Colin took me to Helter Skelter, a shop on Denmark Street in Soho that sold only rock books and magazines. I was excited to finally get to see the shop, because I'd heard of its reputation as an industry hangout. So I started chatting with the owner, Sean, and another man who worked there, telling them of the work I had done for *Mojo* magazine and asking if they knew any of the same people I did.

They didn't say much. But their expressions, and the few words they offered, betrayed the gentle amusement that the British display when humoring people who are overly animated.

Often, at times when I feel awkward or insecure and should really shut up, something in my brain makes me keep talking—as though reeling off more words could make listeners forget the last thing I said. I think that's what happened. I just kept running off the mouth—telling stories, joking, and doing the Loud American thing. And Sean and his employee kept smiling and offering the occasional polite comment.

There was a certain point when I looked over to Colin and saw he had his hands in his pockets and was gazing at the floor with a sullen expression. That's when I realized I had better pay for my books and leave. Until then, I felt I had embarrassed myself, but I embarrass myself so often and in so many ways that it didn't seem like anything worth fretting about.

So, although I could tell Colin wasn't happy with me, the vehemence of his reaction was a shock. No sooner were we outside than he let me have it. I had acted like a fool, he said, embarrassing not only myself but him as well.

My first reaction was to try to placate him: after all, Sean and his co-worker didn't seem to mind my eccentricities. But Colin was having none of it. They were laughing at me the whole time, he said, because I was acting like such an idiot. And he himself was disgusted.

The only thing left for me to do was to offer an apology—only Colin wouldn't accept it.

By the time we arrived back at his house, he had calmed down enough to resume the duties of a host, putting on his videotape of *The Lavender Hill Mob* and watching it with me. But when it came time for bed, he moved himself into his guest room. And he's returned there each night since.

Although the whole situation has me distressed and uncomfortable, I have to admit I was relieved to be sleeping in a different room from Colin on Friday and Saturday nights. That's because two of his children are here for the weekend and I'm glad to avoid causing them distress at seeing their father sharing a bedroom with a woman who's not his wife. It was hard enough for me as a child dealing with my mother's dating; I wouldn't want to inflict that experience on anyone else.

Maybe Colin will warm to me again after his children return to their mother tonight. I hope so.

It was so beautiful to walk along the beach yesterday at Southend with Colin and his grade-school-age kids, who are well-behaved and adorable. Colin parked within view of the seaside, and when we emerged from the car, the first thing I saw was an ancient pub called The Ship. It amazed me, because the plot of the Chesterton novel I am reading—the one I bought beneath Waterloo Bridge—centers upon a pub called The Old Ship.

As Colin and I walked along the sea with his children, I felt a longing to be a maternal presence in their life. The feeling surprised me; I'd never felt anything like it before. I realized I wanted Colin to want me again not only so I could be his wife but also so I could be his children's step-mother.

The children were so sweet, so innocent, that I wanted to protect them. Perhaps that's why I felt so uncomfortable when I saw how Colin was inculcating them with his dark sense of humor.

On the way to and from the seaside resort, whenever we drove past a field of beautiful yellow rapeseed, Colin would lead his children in shouting, "Rape!" I was appalled but kept quiet. And when we passed a church, Colin would make a crack against God and the children would again follow suit.

Upon hearing the first anti-God comment, I felt that as a Jew, even a non-observant one, I had to say something. But I didn't want to embarrass Colin in front of his children. So I only made a mild protest, something lame along the lines of, "Oh, come on now, God's not so bad."

Colin responded matter-of-factly that his was an atheist family. There was nothing for me to do but let it drop.

After we returned to Colin's home in the late afternoon, I went out across the field to the village church to check the times of their Sunday services. It wasn't out of a desire to offend Colin, though I knew he would be disgusted if I associated myself with that place. Something inside me just felt that since Colin was deriding church, that was where I needed to be. Partly I hoped to get something from going to church that I wasn't getting from being with him. Partly I wanted to be different from him, because I wasn't happy with the way he was treating me. Partly I wanted to get out of the house, and nothing else in Ingatestone would be open on a Sunday.

And partly I wanted in some way to make up to God for what Colin had said.

Outside now. A gorgeous, impossibly cloudless day.

The rapeseed is almost as tall as I am. I find the path that runs through it and make my way toward the church. The walk goes by much too quickly and I am in the churchyard amid the medieval graves. There are strange old crypts like nothing I've ever seen, as though some giant passing by had dropped heavy coffins of rough-hewn gray stone onto the grass.

The inside of the church looks medieval too, although the altar area is well lit and the colorful flowers placed there give it a festive air. A grandmotherly usher gives me a *Book of Common Prayer* and a bulletin on which the church's name, St. Edmund and St. Mary, is printed in Old English type. My intuition was correct: even though the place looks Catholic, any church at the center of a British village has to be Church of England.

Glancing around, I see that the crowd is nearly all women, and most of them are in their sixties or older. Also, there are hardly any families with children. But the bulletin says there is a "family service" later in the morning, so perhaps that is when the young couples and kids turn up.

The service begins. I try to sight-sing the hymns. It brings me back to when I was in high school chorus and we performed old Christmas carols.

There are prayers and a few Bible readings; the last one is by the priest, who reads the Gospel. It is all in that King James English with "whither" this and "ye" that. I like the part about the new commandment and loving one another. The world would be a better place if Christians—and everyone—really did that. It will be interesting to hear what the priest has to say about it.

Finally the sermon. That's always been my favorite part of any service, whether the Jewish ones I went to as a kid or the Christian ones I've been to with Mom. I like it so much that I wrote my own sermon when I was six years old, explaining why my sister was wrong in wanting to be president of the world. Because God is president of the world! Go on now, Reverend, inspire me. I need it.

The minister begins by saying that, as the congregation may know, the parish has recently published some bans. His tone has a faint air of embarrassment mixed with disgust. I don't understand. What are they banning?

Ah. *Banns* are news of an upcoming marriage; a furtive glance at the bulletin confirms this. The minister is unhappy because these particular banns are for a famous football player—oh, yes, football means soccer here—who is getting married at this church. And the press is going to come nosing about, and he is sorry that the parish has to put up with it, and he wants to remind everyone to kindly avoid talking to reporters so the couple may have their privacy. Only he, having the British gift for understatement, puts it much more politely than I would.

Now for the sermon. The first word of it is *Lord*. The second is *Sainsbury*. Sainsbury's is a supermarket chain, so Lord

Sainsbury must be the owner. That is the key I need if I am to figure out what the minister is saying . . .

Fifteen minutes later, the minister is still going on and I still don't understand. It is all "Lord Sainsbury" this and "Prime Minister Blair" that. The best I can make out is that Lord Sainsbury has quit his leadership of the supermarket chain in favor of a career in politics, and this is a problem because . . . because why? I can't tell. All I know is that this is more like a BBC news commentary than a *d'var Torah*.

The sermon is finally over. More prayers.

Communion. I don't think I'm supposed to go up, and I wouldn't know what to do anyway. So I stay in my pew and pray the prayers I normally send up at bedtime, asking God to bless and protect me and my family, and to heal my depression. I have no idea what he does with my prayers, if anything; it is just a habit I have had since childhood. If God does hear prayers, it's better to be safe than sorry.

Still more prayers. Another hymn and we are done.

Back outside. Still no clouds.

I had hoped I would feel better now.

Saturday, May 8, 1999, 4:10 p.m. Eeek! I have to leave my apartment in five minutes if I am to make it to the Sidewalk Café by five-fifteen and I don't even have my shoes or jewelry on yet. At least I can put on my makeup while riding the PATH train; goodness knows I've had enough practice.

Since I am having dinner with John Carter, I will have to eat something. Sidewalk has a garden salad; I could probably order that with whole wheat toast, dry, and say I had a late lunch.

Nobody knows I have been starving myself. In March I had a nervous breakdown and stopped wanting to eat. That never happened to me before and it surprised even me. It's especially strange because normally I have what is called "atypical depression," which means, among other things, that I respond to my sadness by eating. But now, thinking about how nobody loves me the way I am, I hate myself so much that I can't bear to eat. Well, my family and friends love me, but no boyfriend loves me.

I know it is stupid to think that stopping eating will really solve anything. There are many women who weigh more than me who have boyfriends and happy lives, so it is probably something within me that makes me so undesirable. But I have never seen what it is like to live as a really thin person, so I would like to experience that now. Also, if being thin doesn't make me happy, I can just continue not eating until I starve myself to death.

Since my breakdown I have lost sixteen pounds. I told my new therapist, who is a kind and caring person, about the breakdown but not the starving part, as I know she would tell me to stop.

The worst part is that people keep telling me how great I look now that I have lost weight. I know they are just trying to be nice, but for me it means they don't care that the reason for my weight loss might be that I am in pain. They don't see that I am crying for help.

Shoes are on now. Size 6½ wide, amazingly enough, down from 8. I had no idea weight loss could affect shoe size, though I guess it makes sense. Earrings and necklace are on, and I am out the door.

Now I am going to forget about my pain for one night. John Carter is performing his first-ever show in New York City, some thirty-five years after he made his name as a hit songwriter, and I made it happen.

I remember when I first met John during my November 1997 London trip. Beach Boys historian Kingsley Abbott, knowing I was a huge fan of his music, brought us together over tea at a Denmark Street café just steps from the building where John and his writing partner Ken Lewis composed hits back in the Sixties.

As I quizzed John about songs he wrote for Herman's Hermits, Manfred Mann, and his own group First Class, I mentioned that my friend Scott claimed the Carter-Lewis composition "Little Bit O' Soul" was actually about God.

My thought was that he would laugh. To my surprise, he answered that Lewis was a fervent Christian; he wrote the lyrics to "Little Bit O' Soul" expressly to see if he could get a song with Gospel references onto the pop charts.

I asked how Lewis was doing. John said he didn't know; they'd had a falling out and hadn't spoken in years.

For some reason that I don't understand, hearing that made me very sad—perhaps sadder than I should have been over goings-on in other people's personal lives.

What hurt me wasn't so much that Carter and Lewis were no longer a songwriting team. It was that they were no longer even friends.

I remember asking John if there was any chance he and Lewis might make up. He responded that he couldn't foresee it ever happening.

Upon returning to the States, I remained in a kind of grief at the thought that Carter and Lewis would never speak again. It grated on me until a few weeks later when I hit upon the idea of asking God to reconcile them.

My stepfather Ron had recently been pressing me to pray for something seemingly impossible, with the idea that I would promise to believe in God if he answered that. It was the same tactic Gary Selman tried on me when I was in college, but this time around I didn't want to take the bait. God might have helped me find Sandy Salisbury, but he wasn't there when I needed the strength to get through the day. I didn't want to ask for a miracle if it meant feeling obliged to believe for the rest of my life even though God might never show his favor to me again.

Be that as it may, one day in December 1997 I felt bad enough over the situation between the former songwriting partners that I gave in and told God I would believe in him provided that "there be a real, positive change in John Carter and Ken Lewis's friendship, so that they reconcile." So now I include that request alongside the prayer I pray every night for God to keep me and my family safe and healthy.

It feels kind of silly to send up a prayer every night when I don't even know for sure whether God hears me. And even if he does hear me, I don't believe he loves me. But I've been doing it on and off since childhood, and old habits are hard to break. Somehow it makes me feel more secure when I'm alone in the dark.

John and I have stayed in touch. I ask him from time to time if he and Lewis have reconciled. The answer is always no.

A few weeks ago, John sent a fax to let me know he would be in New York City for a business meeting. I knew he'd been performing acoustic gigs at a local pub, so I asked if he would be up for doing something similar in the East Village, and wonder of wonders, he said yes. So I scrambled to find a venue. Thankfully, Lach, who books the Fort at Sidewalk Café, had an opening for an evening show.

As simple as that. One day I'm in my apartment feeling sorry for myself and the next I'm aggressively working all my connections to put together a concert for one of my favorite songwriters ever. I earned this night and I am going to enjoy it, even as I dread waking up tomorrow to another day of job-hunting and the struggle to avoid thinking about dying.

About an hour and a half later. At the Sidewalk Café. John didn't ask any questions when I ordered my salad and toast. Good. He also didn't remark on my weight loss or make any comments at all about my appearance, which is also good. Normally I like it when a man notices I've dressed up, but not when he is happily married.

I ask if he's been in touch with Ken Lewis. Yes, he answers—as if it were the most normal thing in the world.

My eyes widen. "So you've *reconciled*?"

"Oh, yes," John nods politely, as though the news were nothing extraordinary.

"That's pretty huge, isn't it? You told me when I met you that you didn't think you and Ken would ever speak to each other again."

"Oh," he says blankly, as though he doesn't quite understand what all the fuss is about. "Well, we're in touch now."

"Wow! That means I have to start believing in God!"

John looks at me, uncomprehending.

I sputter a few words about my promise to God and the daily prayer I have been making for nearly a year and a half. But then I realize that none of this really registers with John, who does not share his former writing partner's penchant for religion. So I change the subject to tonight's show.

Just over an hour later. Full-bodied applause as the sound man introduces John Carter. The efforts I made to get out the word about tonight's show have really paid off. Every table in this small back room of the café is filled.

John sits on a stool, a rented acoustic guitar in his lap. Dressed casually but neatly, with a full head of silver hair and stubbly beard, he looks exactly like what he is: an English rocker who managed to escape the excesses of the psychedelic era.

"I must tell you," he says in his London-via-Birmingham accent, "that some of the songs I'm gonna sing tonight I haven't sung for twenty-five, thirty years. Because these are songs I wrote in the Sixties, and, erm, when you're a songwriter, y'know, and you write a song for someone else and they do it, that's it. You let them do it and you never sing it. So this is going to be a new experience for me as well as you.

"Let's start with something that was a hit for a group over here called the Music Explosion. There were a couple of other interesting versions, by the Ramones and a live version by Tom Petty. This is called 'Little Bit O' Soul.'"

I can't believe this is really happening. This is one of the most distinctive songs of rock's golden era, and it's being played by the man who wrote it, who is sitting ten feet away from me. And he's my friend—even if he might now think I'm a little weird—and I made this concert happen.

"You gotta make like you wanna kneel and pray-ay, yeah," John sings. "Oh, then a little bit o'soul will come your way."

Do I really have to believe now? I so want to believe. I can almost believe for tonight.

But tomorrow—that's the problem. I can't be sure how I'll feel about God tomorrow, because when I wake up, I will still be the same person. And who I am is a girl—a thirty-year-old woman—who hates herself.

My mother loves me. The rest of my family loves me. My friends love me. But who exactly is the me they love? I can't manage to hold onto a worthwhile boyfriend or job. My paying freelance-writing gigs have practically dried up. My apartment is an unholy mess. And I'm so damn sensitive; even minor slights from strangers can make me want to cry or cut myself.

So I can't commit to believing—not because I don't want to, but because it wouldn't be fair to make a promise I can't keep. Dear God, if you want me to believe, you are going to have to make it happen, because I can't do it on my own.

I do feel somehow that, after this answered prayer, it is just a matter of time.

Thursday, May 27, 1999, 1:42 p.m. Inside Mondo Kim's, the creepily fascinating music and video store on St. Mark's Place in the East Village. I have been to this place several times, but normally only to the first floor, where they have good prices on rare imported CDs. But today, having scored a job interview after answering a *Village Voice* ad for a website writer/editor, I walk on past the well-worn poster of Rolling Stones guitarist Brian Jones in Nazi regalia; up the stairs and through the sale-video section; past the display featuring the "Faces of Death" VHS collection ("Banned in 40 Countries!"); up another set of stairs, past the rental-video section with its stock painstakingly organized by genre, director, or photographer; and finally, with the reluctant help of a sullen clerk, up the private elevator to the administrative offices on the fourth floor.

Now I am being led by a young man in a faded Godzilla t-shirt down a bland off-white hallway lit by long fluorescent bulbs that flicker annoyingly. He navigates me past the packing materials and empty boxes cluttering a tiled floor that probably used to be white but is now a dirty gray. Finally he deposits me outside a door next to a large window that affords me a view into the office beyond; I spy a shelf of videos of what look to be obscure arthouse films.

I knock, and a—a man? Yes, this is a man greeting me, although his shape reminds me of the female impersonator

Divine from John Waters's films. He introduces himself as
C.C., webmaster of kimsvideo.com.

C.C. is only a few inches taller than me—probably about
five-foot-six—but it looks like two of me could fit into him.
He wears glasses and has bleached-blonde hair pulled back
in a stubby ponytail that sticks out at an odd angle. And he
seems to have something resembling breasts.

I am prepared to brag to C.C. about how my experience as a writer for Salon.com makes me uniquely quali-
fied for the position, et cetera, et cetera. But I can only
get in a few words before he proceeds to tell me all about
himself.

Five minutes later. I now know that C.C. is gay—
no surprise there—and Palestinian, although he did his
schooling in France. He is also a communist and atheist. The
snapshot that he has taped onto his office window shows
his two sons, ages 6 and 1. He won custody of them after
divorcing their mother, who is "crazy."

Finally, he tells me a little about the job and asks if I have
any questions.

I take a breath and hope my voice will not reveal my
nervousness.

"Well, there is one thing. My résumé gives my name as
Dawn Eden, which is my first and middle name, but my full
name is Dawn Eden Goldstein. You mentioned that you're
Palestinian. Would my being Jewish be a problem?"

"Oh, no!" C.C. assures me, shaking his head.

Tuesday, August 10, 1999, 12:32 p.m. Mom
has that lightness in her voice that tells me she is smiling. I
am speaking to her on my office phone line and have just
confessed to rediscovering the Gideons' pocket-sized New

Testament/Psalms/Proverbs that, since college, has sat on my shelf practically untouched.

"That's great, honey. Which parts have you been reading?"

"Mostly the Psalms," I say in a near-whisper. Even though my office mate Dave has stepped out, the office opens directly into the hall and C.C. could walk by at any moment. "I just page through them and find one that looks interesting."

"And do they help you feel better?" Mom knows what I have been going through at work.

"Well . . ." I hesitate for a moment to think. They do kind of make me feel better, but I don't want to give Mom false hope. "I like them because they remind me that I'm Jewish."

I glance toward the hall and lower my voice as far as I can while remaining audible. "I just feel like, if C.C. hates Jews so much, there must be something good about them."

"Honey, I'm so sorry you have to deal with that. Isn't there *any* other place where you could work? Did you check the ads in the Sunday *New York Times*?"

"Yes, Mom." She can surely tell I'm suppressing a sigh. Nothing gets by her. "This week there was nothing but those temp-agency ads that always turn out to be scams."

"What about applying to the Barnes & Noble in Hoboken?"

"I tried, Mom." For some reason I don't understand, whenever I talk to my mother, practically every other word out of my mouth is *Mom*. "They're not hiring. I have to stay here until I can get another job, because no one will hire me unless I have more full-time experience."

"Well, Ron and I are praying hard for you . . ."

"Excuse me, Mom—Rob, about Victor Mature, don't forget 'Head'! The Monkees movie 'Head'! He played himself, and the Monkees were dandruff in his hair . . .

"Sorry, Mom. Our new online-sales director just walked by and I wanted to give him a tip because he's writing a tribute to Victor Mature, who just died."

"I remember Victor Mature."

"Yeah, well, Mom, can I tell you what C.C. said today?"

"What did he say?"

"He said, '*Your people* just killed a thirteen-year-old Palestinian boy in Hebron.' Every day he says things like that to me. He hates Israel, and I'm just his Jewish punching bag."

"That's horrible."

"And, Mom, he cusses too. And you know—you know how people can have a, what's it called, not a screensaver but a background picture on their computer desktop? Well, he made his background picture a close-up photo of a naked woman, all spread-eagled. It's disgusting, and every time I come into his office it's in my face"

"That's *wrong*! Isn't there anything you can do? Isn't there anyone you can talk to? Can't you talk to his boss?"

"No, Mom, I can't. His boss is Mr. Kim, and Kim's office is set up with a couch and lights—we think he films porn movies in there. Definitely he wouldn't care; he just trusts C.C. to run everything at the website and not bother him."

"We have to find a way to get you out of there."

"Thanks, Mom, I better get going."

"Wait, Dawn, can I tell you one more thing before you go? Just one more thing."

"Sure," I say in the polite tone I use when I really want to get off the phone. C.C. just walked by and he knows my lunch break should be over by now.

"What is happening to you is *spiritual warfare*. You are being persecuted by the spirit of the Evil One."

"Yes." I would be annoyed with Mom right now for getting all religious on me if what she was saying were not so obviously true.

"Do you have a pen? I want to give you something to write down."

"Sure."

"Are you ready?"

"Yes."

"Psalm twenty-seven."

I repeat the number and Mom continues: "If you pray that psalm every day, it will give you strength. What you need right now is spiritual protection."

"Okay, Mom. Thanks." Out of the corner of my eye, I see C.C. enter the hall by my office. He stops and scowls at me. "Will do. Gotta go. Bye."

8

I'm a Believer

Thursday, September 30, 1999, 9:48 a.m.
Crap! Not my favorite word, but it fits my mood. I am already eighteen minutes late to work and have not even made it across Cooper Square. And the rain is pouring down, and the three-dollar umbrella I just purchased from an opportunistic street vendor already has two spokes jutting out. The final leg of my morning commute—a walk eastward from the Ninth Street PATH station to Kim's—has become a game of strategy as I struggle to avoid either drenching my new black patent-vinyl heels in a garbage-clogged gutter or poking a fellow pedestrian in the eye.

It was stupid of me to waste time putting on black cake eyeliner before leaving for the office. Normally I don't wear eyeliner except when going to nightclubs. But ever since Rob came on board as Kim's online-sales director, I have wanted to dress up for work.

It's funny, because Rob is so not my type. He has a beard—
I can't see the point of beards; all they do is cover up a man's
face. Plus he is slightly younger than me, and I haven't found
a younger man attractive in a few years. At least, not since
Steve, that sweet drummer in London who looked like a taller version of Alec Guinness in "Great Expectations."

But I can't help liking Rob. He's from New Jersey, like
me, and proud of it, and he reminds me of the guys I hung
out with in high school and college who were into weird
pop culture from the Sixties and Seventies. He even has his
own filmzine, *Vex*; its tagline is, "Movies Hate You." The
first time we had a one-on-one conversation in the office, he
gave me a copy of an issue featuring an encyclopedic article
on the history of movies featuring men in gorilla suits. Its
headline was "The Apes of Wrath."

And Rob likes me, too, at least enough to leave the office
with me for lunch sometimes—though it could just be that
he too wants to get away from C.C., who is getting more
eccentric by the day.

Coming up to Astor Place now. How could Starbucks
open a second café within view of the one that was already
here? Counting the one inside the Astor Place Barnes &
Noble, that makes three Starbucks on one block. Insane!
The Village I love is turning into a shopping mall.

What is C.C. going to do today? I don't want to think
about it. And I'm not sure how much weirder he can get
since his bizarre feat this past Monday. That's when he made
a great show of evicting himself from his own office—the
largest on the floor save for Mr. Kim's. He gave the room to
Rob and moved himself into a storage closet down the hall.

I think I know the reason for C.C.'s munificence. His
office was next to Mr. Kim's, and he wanted to get as far
away from his boss as possible. In any case, he hauled his

computer—which he never seemed to use, save to look at the splayed-out nudie on its desktop—into the closet and hooked up a crane lamp.

Yes, it was bizarre. Even my most jaded co-workers, who have seen enough craziness for a few lifetimes, were creeped out.

Five minutes later. Whew! C.C. didn't see me come in. Maybe he won't find out how late I am. I can trust Dave not to tell him.

Dave, a middle-aged Englishman, is already in his seat at the long desk we share, perusing some notes he's jotted down on a legal pad.

"Morning!" I say.

Dave lifts his eyes from the pad. "We had a meeting today—me, C.C., and Rob—about the new marketing plan for the website. Mr. Kim wants us to get something together quickly because Amazon just launched its zedshops."

"Its what?"

"I think they're called zedshops?" Dave checks his legal pad.

"Oh, zShops!" I chuckle. Even though Dave has lived in the States for years, he still talks like he's just arrived from England. "Right. I read about that in today's *Times*. It's something that enables small merchants to sell on Amazon."

"Right. Well, Rob had all these ideas about videos he wants to sell."

Dave pauses. His expression turns serious. "It's strange stuff."

"Like what?"

"People having holes drilled into their head . . ." He checks his notes. "Trepanation, I think he said . . ."

"*What?*"

Dave looks at the legal pad again. "People drinking their own urine . . ."

"He must have been joking."

My jaw has dropped a bit but my officemate doesn't see it; his eyes are still on his notes. "He wants to sell videos of women throwing up."

"No." My eyes are bugging out. "No way."

"That's what they want to do with the site." Dave's voice has a hint of resignation. "You can ask Rob."

"I will!"

Oops. I shouldn't have raised my voice. Dave means well and I'm not agitated at him personally. Probably I should apologize to him. But it's too late; I've already marched myself across the hall into Rob's—formerly C.C.'s—office.

Rob is finishing up a phone call. I stand and wait, looking around to see how he has decorated the office. As I would expect, there are some posters for trashy films. But other than that, it looks pretty much the same as when C.C. was in residence.

The gigantic gray-brown metal file cabinet is still there against the wall. Probably it is too heavy to move. I wonder what's in it. It looks older than the video store itself.

"OK, great. Talk to you later. Bye." Rob hangs up the receiver and looks up at me with an open face.

I take a breath. "Rob . . ."

For a second all I can do is stare into the middle distance. How do I even begin?

Another breath. "What's this I hear about some weird videos you want to sell on the site? Like a video about people getting holes in their skull?"

Rob smiles. "You mean *A Hole in the Head*."

"What's the deal with that?"

"It's a documentary that appeared on the Learning Channel last year about trepanation. There's a whole history behind it."

"Oh."

I pause to process this new bit of information. A legitimate documentary about a historical practice. Well, all right.

"And people drinking their own urine?"

"Same thing. It's a documentary about people who do that for health reasons. They say it boosts their immunity."

"Oh." It takes me a moment to process that too.

"Also . . . what's this about videos of women throwing up?"

Rob lets out a chuckle. "I got this insane catalog."

Reaching over to the corner of his desk, he picks up a color pamphlet and hands it to me. "It's got all this wild stuff. We're going to promote some of these videos on the front page of the site to draw attention to our online shopping."

Before I can peruse the catalog, C.C. appears in the doorway. It's clear he wants Rob's attention.

I turn to Rob. "Can I look at this?"

"Sure."

Wriggling past C.C., I hightail it back across the hall to my office.

Dave has stepped out, which is a relief as I don't really want anyone to see me looking at the catalog.

It's no surprise to me that Rob's job includes ensuring that pornographic videos are promoted on the website. Everybody knows that much of Kim's business, both in-store and online, comes from its voluminous porn and "sexploitation" inventory.

But just from the catalog's front page, I can tell it is beyond anything I have ever seen or heard about before.

It is from a company that distributes videos targeted at viewers who have sexual fetishes. Judging by the photos on the cover, the distributor specializes in videos of surgically enhanced women who are vomiting, or at least pretending to vomit.

The cover features a large photo of a tall, white woman with a stringy mane of shopping-mall hair in a bright green string bikini and open-toed gold stilettos. She stands pigeon-toed, facing the camera, her hands cupped over her silicone breasts, her eyes crossed in Ben Turpin fashion. Her cheeks are stuffed with something; they look as round as her breasts.

Beneath the large photo is a smaller one, a sort of "after" shot. It shows the same woman with gunk spewing out of her mouth.

I march back into Rob's office—no sign of C.C. now—and drop the catalog back onto his desk, wishing it were a used barf bag. "You're not really going to put this on the front page, are you?"

"Mr. Kim and C.C. love it. It's part of the marketing plan."

"But . . . but . . ." I sputter. "Why do we need to market this? It's demeaning toward women."

"Oh, come on!" Rob laughs. "This isn't demeaning toward women," he says as he reaches for the catalog. Now he is holding it up. "This is demeaning to *human beings*. Look at it!"

He looks at it himself. "It's *stupid*," he adds—pushing out his lips to lengthen the "u" so it comes out *stoopid*. "And it's funny."

Satisfied he has made his point, he turns his gaze back to me. "You can't take it so seriously."

My heart begins to race. I stare at Rob, incredulous, until the words come out. "It's *funny*? You think that women getting sick is funny?"

With each sentence, my voice escalates louder and higher. Now it is a tortured whine. "You think it's funny when women are in pain?"

Rob grins nervously. "Come on, Dawn . . ."

He's not going to placate me. I am in the zone. "You want to make money from women in pain . . . because you think it's funny?"

But Rob refuses to wipe the grin off his face. Probably he thinks if he keeps grinning I'll just give up and leave his office in disgust. Or maybe he's trying to provoke me to show I can cuss like everyone else in this godforsaken place.

"Why does it matter?" he shrugs. "None of this matters."

My eyes bulge. "It matters because they're human beings!" I yell. "It matters because . . ."

Suddenly I feel exhausted, wiped. The adrenaline moment has peaked; now I am short of breath and want to cry. But I have to finish the thought. "It matters if anyone, anywhere hurts."

Rob doesn't offer a reply, but his grin is finally gone. Its disappearance gives me my confidence back. "You don't care, do you? You don't care if women are hurt so you can sell your stupid videos."

"Yeah," Rob says, getting tired of this game. "Yeah, that's right, I don't care."

"All right," I gasp. "All right. You don't think it matters if someone gets hurt. Well, I'm going to prove it to you that it does matter—even if I have to hurt myself—"

Now it's Rob's turn to gasp as I pull back my right arm—

"*Bam! Bam! Bam! on the metal file cabinet!*" I scream—punctuating each "bam" with the sound of my bare forearm hitting the side of the gray-brown metal monstrosity, full force. It makes for a loud, reverberating crash. Each time.

All Rob's irony evaporates. "Please, stop. Please, stop."

Really and truly exhausted now, to the point of panting. But still hitting that monster, though with diminishing force. "Bam . . . bam . . . wow, that hurt . . ."

I am peering myopically at my forearm, trying to see if the skin is broken, when C.C. storms in. The sound of my bams must have reached his little broom closet.

"What are you doing?" he bellows. "Do you know that I could hear you all the way down the hall? I could have you fired."

That's C.C.'s favorite weapon in his arsenal, suitable for transgressions large and small: the old "I could have you fired." He made that threat when he caught me reading employment ads on the job. And he made it when I yawned during a meeting after being up all night writing up my Guided by Voices interview for Salon.com. I would roll my eyes if I weren't in pain.

"I'm sorry . . ." I mutter, staring at my throbbing forearm and flexing my fingers to make sure they all still work—they do. Whew! It's my writing hand.

With my left hand, I cradle my right forearm against my chest. The bones in my forearm are still vibrating from the impact of the wallops, and there's a stinging pain in the place where my skin hit the sharp edge of the cabinet's side. C.C. and Rob stare as I stagger out of Rob's office and back across the hall to my desk.

About six hours later. Somehow I have managed to get some writing and editing done today, though not as much as usual, given that I am using only my left hand.

Right now I am just finishing my capsule biography/filmography of Agnes Varda, written with much help from Alltheweb.com and the various reference books lying around the office. That leaves Lina Wertmüller for tomorrow.

Once I write up Wertmüller, the name of every female director listed on kimsvideo.com will be hyperlinked to a paragraph of original content about her work. Then C.C.

will give me another list. It would be nice if it were some-thing closer to my line of interest, such as silent movies, screwball comedies, or Sixties rock films. But most of what I like has too little sex and violence for Kim's customers. Already on this job I have learned more than I care to know about spaghetti westerns, Hong Kong action films, and Jap-anese anime.

My right forearm rests upon what was a bag of ice and is now just a soggy bag of ice water wrapped in paper towels. Rob surprised me by bringing it in a short while after our confrontation; he had bought the ice from a vendor down the street. He informed me that he could have insisted I be fired, but he wasn't going to do so.

I wasn't crazy about Rob's self-satisfied tone; he made no apology for his insistence on promoting "stoopid" videos. But I wanted to keep my job, so I thanked him for his for-bearance as well as for the ice.

"Hey."

I swivel around to find Rob standing behind me.

"Hey," I echo.

"How's your arm?"

I lift my arm off the ice pack and try it out. "It feels fine."

"Wow. I thought for sure you had fractured it."

"I don't think so," I say, looking at it. There is a faint scratch at the spot where I hit the edge of the cabinet. Other than that, there is no sign that anything happened to it at all.

"Wow. OK. I'm heading out."

"See you tomorrow."

Six and a half hours later. How many weeks has it been since I last changed my sheets? Three? I can see the fingerprint stains on the bottom sheet from when I ate Cheez Doodles a few nights ago. But it's too late at night and I'm too tired to change the sheets or put away my clean laundry or bag up my dirty laundry or clear out the dishes from the sink or put away the CDs, cassettes, and vinyl records that are scattered haphazardly atop the gray-tinted plastic dustcover that protects my turntable.

And of course there is no hope of ever clearing out the assorted boxes and bins with their concert flyers, correspondence, and yellowing magazines, let alone the piles of loose papers that cover nearly every available surface area. God knows I've tried. Every paper is important and meaningful and deserves to be filed, only the act of filing them would require sitting down and thinking about my past: men I loved, or thought I loved; friendships that have dissipated; bands that have broken up; people who have died; clothes I used to fit into. And I really don't feel like doing that. Ever.

This looks like the apartment of a depressed person who is overwhelmed with life. Well, so be it. It is. I'm going to bed.

Before switching off the light, I re-examine my arm. It feels perfectly normal, with no pain whatsoever. The bones aren't sore and it doesn't seem like I've torn any muscles. Most surprisingly, there is no bruising—only that faint scratch.

In the past, I have endured blows far less dramatic that had far more dramatic effects. All it takes is some yuppie to hit my shin with his briefcase on the PATH train and I'm black and blue for weeks. But to have almost no effects from hitting, full force, a file cabinet that is built like an army tank—that is downright miraculous.

Maybe God likes what I did. Even though it was foolish and embarrassing.

The light is off now. I sit up in bed, watching the shadow on my wall cast by the telephone pole outside. It moves to and fro with the headlights of passing traffic. A faint siren wails in the distance.

Along the opposite wall from my bed, above the shelves housing my stereo, I can see the outlines of the giant plastic treble clef and music notes I tacked up. They were manufactured as music-teacher supplies; I put them up a few years ago because their kitschy and vaguely retro look went with the shabby-chic mood I was going for. That was back when I still thought there was a possibility I might one day make my apartment look presentable.

"Dear God," I pray out loud in a hurried monotone, "thank you for keeping me and my loved ones safe and healthy today."

Those initial words roll off my tongue easily. I have been praying them pretty much every night since childhood, though at some point I must have stopped reeling off a list of family and friends, opting instead to lump them all together into "loved ones." God has never talked back, but in a superstitious way I feel safer talking to him than I would if I just went straight to bed.

"Please keep us all safe and healthy this coming day." Oops, forgot it's just after midnight. "*Today.*"

"And, dear God," I add—my voice gaining a bit more emotion because I'm now ad-libbing—"please don't let me be fired. If I have to lose my job, please let it be because I'm laid off but not because I'm fired."

I ask this because I know I'm not good at lying. If, after being fired, I interviewed for another job, my potential employer would want to know why I was no longer at Kim's, and I would have to tell the truth. But if I were laid off, I could honestly say that the fault wasn't mine; Kim's had simply cut back on staff.

Got to sign off now. I'm sleepy. "Thank you, God. According to your will," I add, remembering Del Shannon's admonition. Has it really been ten years? I miss Del.

Thursday, October 7, 1999, 9:31 a.m. I had hoped to make it from the employee elevator at Kim's to my office down the hall without having to run into C.C., but it's too late. He just now stuck his head out of his comical hole-in-the-wall office, asking me to find two of my co-workers and bring them along with myself to see him.

Whatever news he has for us, it can't be good. His face looked ashen.

I round up the co-workers. We stand in the hallway by C.C.'s open door since his office has barely enough room for himself, let alone visitors.

C.C. takes a breath. His expression is still grave.

"I'm very sorry to tell you this, but I have bad news. This morning, Mr. Kim told me that we have to downsize our website staff. In the immediate future, that means we're stopping work on our film database. All our resources are going to be turned toward developing online sales.

"So I have to lay you off. I'm very sorry."

I feel a cheer welling up in my bosom. My eyes start to widen with what would be a burst of joy—but I catch myself just in time and let my face fall.

C.C. looks so sad. I have to let him have his moment.

He really believes he stands for the working people—even though he constantly abuses them. He can fire someone capriciously and not think twice about it. But being forced to lower the axe on innocent workers because of the selfish capitalist whims of a petty oligarch is more than he can handle.

"I'm hoping we'll be able to hire you back once the site starts to make money," C.C. concludes.

I nod with the best fake sincerity I can muster, thank him, and head down the hall to my office. Then I wait as C.C. arranges for me to receive my final pay envelope—which I know will contain, as usual, not an actual paycheck but cash.

Eight minutes later. Heading back downstairs in the employee elevator. It's a good thing I don't need a key to make it go down, as I just returned mine to C.C.

The doors open on the main floor and I stride out—past the imported Sonic Youth vinyl records, past the gray t-shirts bearing the cryptic legend "blur: are shite," past the walls papered with flyers for concerts at Coney Island High and CBGB—and into the bright East Village morning.

My prayers have been answered. I wasn't fired. I was laid off. I am free!

Wednesday, October 20, 1999, 10:43 p.m. Staring at a blank Microsoft Word page on my Blueberry iMac with no idea of what to type on it. Meanwhile, the voice coming through my stereo speakers is shouting, "You're a monk, I'm a monk, we're all monks!"

I must be getting old. The Monks are touted as the first punk band. But to me, their music just sounds like noise. It's little more than a bunch of guys shouting over fuzzed-out guitars and a double-time beat.

But my new friend Joshua was kind enough to assign me to write a preview of the Monks' upcoming NYC reunion appearances for his arts website Offoffoff.com. And I do want to promote the band, if only because I have a soft spot for Sixties rockers who get back in the game. Plus they deserve credit for bucking the tide. At a time when other bands boasted Beatle haircuts and matching suits, the Monks sported tonsures and habits.

Finally the words begin to flow:

The Monks, a group of ex-G.I.'s who recorded in Germany during the mid-1960s, were loud, rude, sophomoric, and atonal. In other words, ahead of their time.

Writing takes my mind off my fear that my mood will spiral down to the lowest ebb of my cyclical suicidal depression. On a normal day, I wish I didn't have to wake up the next morning, but I don't feel like doing anything to prevent such an occurrence. But once my mood starts to head downward—which could happen at any time, without notice—I am in real danger of acting on my suicidal feelings. And the downward part of the cycle can last for weeks.

Once the exhilaration of being let go from Kim's wore off, the possibility that my self-destructive urges might return became my biggest worry, especially with the stress of job-hunting.

Kim's was awful, but it enabled me, for the first time in years, to escape financial reliance upon Mom and Dad. Now, if I want to stay independent, I not only have to scan the employment ads—which are for unspeakably dull positions like a "cutting-edge online editor" at *Chemical Week*—but also return to freelancing. That means reconnecting with my editorial contacts at music magazines—very few of whom return my emails, as I've been out of touch with them for months. When they do, they typically say they don't have openings because they have to keep their current freelancers busy.

Thankfully, my downstairs neighbor Irwin introduced me to Offoffoff editor Joshua, so at least I have one new paying outlet. Joshua, who writes headlines for the *New York Post* by day, offers $25 for previews of upcoming New York City events, which is pretty decent considering he only needs 250 words. I can write a piece for him in a few hours and it enables me to eat takeout for a day.

What's more, Joshua is my type—big soulful eyes, tall, witty, sensitive, overeducated—though he doesn't seem interested in me as more than a friend. Plus he has a girlfriend. He mentioned her in conversation this afternoon when we met up at Castle Point Park, walking the same paths where Marlon Brando's character wooed that of Eva-Marie Saint in *On the Waterfront*.

It was a lovely brisk autumn day, perfect for a deep philosophical conversation as we wandered amid the falling leaves. Joshua opened up about his background and I was impressed at how it was similar to mine; Reform Jewish upbringing, divorced parents, straight-laced father, bohemian mother. Like me, he had fallen away from the faith, only he was a Sinophile and was interested in Buddhism.

I told him that, although I didn't go for Eastern religion or anything involving meditation, I'd had some experiences that made me wonder about a world beyond my perception.

A few years ago, on and off over a period of months, I'd experienced some nighttime disturbances. I would wake up finding myself unable to move a muscle. It felt like being buried alive.

The paralysis was always accompanied by the terrifying certainty that there was a presence in the room. Although it was an interior certainty, it was usually amplified by some outside sensation, such as the bed shaking or a breeze inexplicably blowing back and forth over my face.

All I could think about on such occasions was that I had to wake up fully or I would die. Somehow, after a brief struggle, I would manage to shake myself awake and be free. When I did, I would find there was no one else in the room but me.

Eventually, I said to Joshua, I learned through a website that there was a medical term for what I experienced: *hypnopompic sleep paralysis*. Perhaps my experiences were caused by one of the mood medications I was on. But at the time they took place, I couldn't shake the idea that they were supernatural.

It's strange that the memory of those experiences came up during my conversation with Joshua. I hardly ever mention them to anyone. There was just that one time when I told some friends from the music scene about a particularly frightening sleep-paralysis episode. They, however, found it hilarious. From then on, I decided to keep such stories to myself. But there was something spiritual about Joshua that made me feel safe opening up to him.

Must stop thinking about Joshua now. He's not interested. If I let myself obsess on him, it could destroy me. There is nothing I want more than to be loved by a man, really loved. Nothing. Not even my dream job.

I almost wish Joshua lived in London or Los Angeles, someplace where I could have a whirlwind romance with him that we both knew wouldn't go anywhere. At least then I could have the experience of making love to him. Well, it wouldn't really be love if we barely knew each other, but at least I could have a more real experience of the fantasy of being in love with him. I would know how he kisses and what he says and does when he is making love, and it would tell me something about what he is like when he lets himself be vulnerable.

But he lives less than a mile from me—no two places in Hoboken are more than a mile apart. And even if I could convince him to have sex with me, I would then have to see him on the PATH train and know he is never really going to love me. Plus my pushing myself on him would wreck our writer/editor relationship and, if he's serious about wanting to be my friend, it would wreck our friendship as well.

So I can't let myself think too hard about him. It would only push me into the tailspin I dread.

It really is amazing that I've been out of a job for two weeks and have not yet succumbed to sadness. I can't explain it. It's almost as miraculous as my arm being preserved unharmed after I smashed it against Rob's file cabinet.

Friday, October 22, 1999, 5:04 a.m. Oh, no. Here we go again.

I am in bed. I am—I *was* asleep. Only now I am awake— at least, I *think* I'm awake, unless this is a dream—and I can't move. And there is a roaring in my ears.

Forty-three minutes later. As I sit at my computer, wearing my ratty pink-and-white terrycloth bathrobe, I know it is far too early to be up. But I am too unsettled to go back to bed.

I open my Eudora email program to begin a message— *Dear Joshua, Guess what happened?*—when I feel a chill coming on and I have to go to the bathroom again.

Back at my iMac now. Too exhausted to type, so I just huddle over the screen and stare. *Guess what happened?* What did happen?

That roaring that was in my ears—I know what that was. It was the blood rushing. I've had that happen before in sleep paralysis; it makes me hear bodily sounds that I don't hear in waking life.

But what was that screeching? That wasn't a noise from inside my body. That sound came from outside. It sounded like some strange bird, and it was loud enough to jolt me awake.

It takes me some time to review in my mind the potential causes of the bizarre high-pitched noise. Finally I recall that, while suffering the sleep paralysis, I was trying to gasp for breath, only I couldn't even move my jaw.

So I would have gasped through clenched teeth. Is that even possible?

I try it now. My lips pucker as I suck in the air through the gaps between my teeth, resulting in an inverted whistle.

Well, now I know what were the noises I heard. But what else happened?

I'm not sure. There was a presence. Something, someone, besides me was in the room.

About twelve hours later. Glad I managed to fall back asleep this morning. Otherwise I might have slept during the hour-long train ride to Morristown and missed my stop. My stepfather and I are going to see *Naked Gun* star Leslie Nielsen in his touring one-man show as Clarence Darrow.

Right now I am at the dinner table listening to Mom and Ron talk animatedly about Melchizedek. They are interested in him because his name comes up in the Torah reading for this week, *Lech-Lecha*. Although they believe in Jesus, Ron wants to maintain participation in the Jewish community, so they worship at a local synagogue every Saturday morning.

Now they are talking about how Melchizedek represents Jesus. Of course. Everything in the Bible represents Jesus to them—well, everything good, anyway.

I let them talk, as I'm much more interested in communing with the cornflake-fried chicken nuggets that Ron made tonight—my favorite. It's a relief to be well enough to eat after all that happened this morning.

Suddenly I blurt out, "Some things are not meant to be known. Some things are meant to be understood."

Ron turns to me. "What?"

"Where is that in the Bible? It's got to be in the Bible?"

"What?"

"'Some things are not meant to be known. Some things are meant to be understood.' I heard that. I heard it this morning, when I had that feeling I told you about, where I was frozen in bed and it felt like someone was in the room."

"I remember it now," I go on. "There was a voice. A woman's voice. I know it sounds crazy.

"She spoke slowly and deliberately, like this," and I repeat the words.

"That's got to be in the Bible somewhere," I conclude. "Where is it?"

If anyone can find anything in the Bible, they can. Lord knows they've quoted it to me thousands of times over the years during their practically nonstop efforts to convert me.

"I don't know," says Mom. "Ron, do you know?"

"I don't, but we can look it up when we get back. Right now we've got to start getting ready to leave if we're going to make it to the show."

Three and a half hours later. Riding home with Ron and agreeing with him about how heavy-handed the show was. Hope Mom is still up. When we left, she said she was about to lie down; she felt a migraine coming on.

Just as Ron pulls the SUV into the driveway, I exclaim, "Romans 5:1! That's where it is in the Bible. I have to look up Romans 5:1!"

The verse just came to me, out of nowhere, yet I know it's the one I'm looking for. I just know.

Ron parks and I spring out the car door to dash in ahead of him.

"Hi, Mom, we're home!"

Mom pokes her head out of her and Ron's bedroom, still woozy from her migraine. "Oh, hi, honey, how was the show?"

"Romans 5:1," I say, half to my mother and half to myself. "I have to look up Romans 5:1."

Before she can point me to a Bible, I'm off to find one myself. It shouldn't be too hard; they're all over the house. Certainly the living room will have one.

There's one on the coffee table. I kneel down on the rug to pick it up, opening it at the New Testament end, and flip around until I find what I'm looking for.

Well, that's a comedown.

"Did you find it?"

I look up to see Ron standing in the doorway. "Yes. It's interesting—I'm sure it's an important verse—but it's not what I heard in my dream."

"What is it?"

"'Therefore being justified by faith, we have peace with God through our Lord Jesus Christ.' What does 'justified' mean?"

It's embarrassing to have to ask the meaning of a simple word, and especially to have to ask Ron. He may be smart, but I can beat him in Scrabble any day. And I do know what *justified* means in ordinary conversation. But with Mom out of commission, I need his help to discover if the word has some special biblical meaning that I am not understanding.

In any case, Ron is delighted to be consulted. He pulls down from a shelf some dusty old books bulky enough to be doorstops and explains to me that they are concordances. They contain the meanings of Bible words along with listings of all the places in the Bible where they occur.

Strong's Concordance says the Greek word for *justified* in the New Testament comes from a verb meaning to "make righteous." So what, if anything, does it have to do with knowledge and understanding?

Ron suggests I look to see where else the word is used. So I go down the list of references to other instances of the word in Romans. Finally I find one that mentions knowledge: Romans 3:20: "Therefore by the deeds of the law there shall no flesh be justified in his sight: for by the law is the knowledge of sin."

I read over the passage a few times and read the verses around it to get a better feel.

"So," I muse, "law is knowledge, but law doesn't justify. And faith does. Would that make faith equivalent to understanding rather than mere knowledge?"

"That's right!" Ron exclaims. He is so happy.

And maybe, I think to myself, God is trying to tell me that all this time I have been trying to find him through exterior knowledge—through proofs, like answered prayers—I need instead to have the understanding that comes through faith. And that this understanding is something that is more than externals; it's something inside.

So, if some things are not meant to be known but are meant rather to be understood, then if I entrust myself to God in faith—in understanding—then the knowledge will be added to me.

That actually makes sense.

I rise from the rug and plant myself at one end of the nearby couch. Ron takes the other end and I tell him what I am thinking.

"The thing is," I add, "if that's what God means—if he wants me to make this leap of faith so that he can then give me the knowledge—I just wish he would actually come and speak to me." Remembering that Ron says he's had mystical experiences, I add, "Like he did with you."

"But, Dawn, you don't understand. He already *has*!" Ron exclaims. "That's what happened to you last night."

"But that was a woman's voice."

"It doesn't matter. It's still from God."

I pause to reflect.

"I guess . . ." I say, thinking out loud, "I guess God can speak with a woman's voice if he wants to."

"Of course he can."

I start to laugh. It becomes a loud, rolling laugh, filled with joy. Ron laughs too.

Mom emerges from the bedroom at the sound of our laughter, looking surprised and pleased. "What's so funny?"

It takes me a moment to collect myself and get the words out.

"Mom, I have to believe in Jesus now!"

At least, I think I have to. There have been too many signs not to try.

About an hour later. It feels so embarrassing to get down on my knees beside my bed with a Gideons Bible in my hand, even though there is no one to see me—no one except God. But I asked Mom what I was supposed to do next, and she said I had to get down on my knees, pray the Sinner's Prayer, and ask Jesus to come into my heart. So I can't go to sleep until I do it.

The prayer is inside the front cover. Here goes:

Confessing to God that I am a sinner, and believing that the Lord Jesus Christ died for my sins on the Cross and was raised for my justification, I now receive and confess Him as my personal Savior.

There's that word again—"justification."

Saturday, October 23, 1999, 9:15 a.m. That sound. I know that sound.

Ah, yes. It's the sound of the alarm clock—now switched off. I am at my mother's and stepfather's house and have been in a deep sleep. And I said the Sinner's Prayer before going to bed.

Rising to sit for a moment in bed before getting up, I don't feel that joyful spirit I felt last night, when Ron and I were laughing. But still, I feel . . . different.

Something has changed. But what?

Do I still wish I were dead? Not that I would do anything about it, but do I still wish it?

No. I don't. And I don't because I can't.

I can't wish I were dead anymore. I can't even think about harming myself. Because God loves me. He created me, so he must have a purpose for keeping me alive. And Jesus is his Son.

From now on, I have to learn to be happy.

Tuesday, July 31, 2001, 12:23 p.m. "This song is about people who are no longer here. They've passed over . . . to the other side."

With those words, Dave Davies plays the raga-rock riff that kicks off "See My Friends," one of the most haunting songs his brother Ray has ever written.

"See my friends, see my friends, playin' 'cross the river . . ."

I can't believe I am actually onstage with the Kinks' guitarist. Well, all right, I'm not actually performing with him but only standing in the wings next to a handful of red plastic chairs set up for concert employees and friends of the band. But still, there he is, the great Dave Davies, playing his heart out just twenty feet away from me.

And there they are, thousands of people grooving to the music in the bright Manhattan summer sun, men and women of all ages, a few families with kids. Scattered through the crowd are some men in button-down shirts and ties;

they must be glad for a chance to rock out during their lunch break from their desk jobs at Morgan Stanley or wherever they work up there in the towers.

The Twin Towers. I turn my gaze upward to see them looming amazingly high, watching over us like sparkling sentinels.

"She is gone," Dave sings. "She is gone and now there's no one left . . ."

What a blessing it is to do publicity for Summer Hits, the series of free oldies concerts at the World Trade Center, helping make it possible for people to have such beautiful shared experiences. And to think I once feared that, upon becoming a Christian, I would have to write off my past life as a rock historian as one big waste. Nothing is wasted with God.

Best of all, Ray and Steve, the promoters of Summer Hits' parent series, CenterStage at the World Trade Center, say there's a good chance they'll be able to hire me back next summer. And who knows—they might even engage my help during the rest of the year at other venues they book. How wonderful it would be to do this for the rest of my life.

Monday, September 10, 2001, 7:43 p.m. This is the first time I've been in an apartment in Manhattan's Hell's Kitchen since I interviewed singer Lou Christie at his townhouse a few years back. But Bob Paolucci's apartment is far more modest than that of the Sixties pop legend. It's a typically cramped Manhattan railroad flat, suitable for a former monk turned translator.

Even so, Bob's hospitality more than makes up for what he lacks in luxury. He does everything he can to make his fellow members of the New York City G.K. Chesterton Society feel at home. I especially like that he dispenses drinks in golden goblets—or chalices, as the Catholics here call them.

When I saw this group listed on the American Chesterton Society website's directory, I hoped it might be a way for me to find a boyfriend who shares my interests. But although men outnumber women among the dozen or so attendees, I don't see anyone who is boyfriend material, at least not at first glance.

The only man here who is close to my age looks too conventional to be interested in a Jewish-born rock historian. Also, he is probably Catholic, in which case he *really* wouldn't be interested in me. In fact, as far as I can tell, everyone here is Catholic except for me.

Oh well. At least there is Christian community here, which is something I really need. And I do believe Catholics are Christians, although I'm not sure if the worshipers at the Hoboken Faith Community Fellowship, where I was baptized, would agree. Somewhere in one of the booklets they gave me, I read that the Catholic Church is the Whore of Babylon. Well, Jesus hung out with whores too.

I will always be grateful to the Hoboken Faith Community Fellowship for granting me my request for a "generic baptism" when I came to them as a new believer. Under their kind pastor's guidance, I was baptized simply in the name of the Father, and of the Son, and of the Holy Spirit, without having to profess the Adventist teachings they believed. But given my unwillingness to enter their denomination, I knew I would never really fit in with that community.

When people ask me what I am, I tell them I'm Evangelical or born-again. Sometimes I'll say I'm a Jewish believer, but that comes out only when I'm around Christians who are uncomfortable with Jews or Judaism. It feels good, in a mean kind of way, to set them off balance, forcing them to confront their prejudices.

Actually, I shouldn't get pleasure from that. That's wrong. I'm sorry, Jesus. Please change me.

Anyway, if I am going to grow as a Christian, what I really need is a church home. And I just haven't found a place where I feel like I belong. One church has bad sermons; another has bad hymns; one is unattractive; another is unfriendly; one is too far away; and so on.

In fact, come to think of it, finding the right church is almost as challenging as finding the right boyfriend. No, cancel that, it *is* as challenging, and in both cases I would despair if I didn't believe God was in charge.

So, not being part of a worship community, it really is a pleasure at least to be able to sit with fellow Christians for a couple of hours and discuss an author I love. Best of all, tonight we are discussing *The Man Who Was Thursday.*

Kevin, who is married—but I'm really not too disappointed about that, as he has a moustache—is talking about how Chesterton's readers would have responded to his depiction of a secret group of anarchists plotting to throw a bomb.

"How serious was the danger of anarchism at the time Chesterton was writing?" I ask. Gosh, it feels so good just to be able to mention G.K. Chesterton in conversation with people who know what I'm talking about.

"Well," Kevin responds, "at the time Chesterton was writing, in 1907, anarchists were a genuine threat. People lived in fear of someone throwing a bomb. A comparison for us would be the fear of radical Muslim terrorists."

"Like that sheikh who masterminded the bombing of the World Trade Center back in —was it 1994?" I remember the day of the bombing as the day I saw Gene Pitney sing at Carnegie Hall, but I can't recall which year that was.

John, the graying gent seated a couple of chairs to my right, pipes up. "Ninety-three. You're thinking of the blind sheikh, Omar Abdel-Rahman."

"That's right," I say, trying to sound as though the name had just been on the tip of my tongue. It's intimidating to be among people who are so much more knowledgeable than I am about history and current events. I spent so many years filling my memory with trivia about Sixties pop that there wasn't much room left to retain information of interest to educated people.

John is going on about the Islamists' effort to destroy the World Trade Center, and he is linking it to something called Lepanto. But I'm not paying attention because the mention of the World Trade Center makes me wistful. How I wish I were going to work at a concert there tomorrow, just as I did every Tuesday from June through August. But now the CenterStage series is done for the year, and Ray and Steve are resting from their labors. I need to wait at least another two weeks before I can nudge them to give me more work.

Friday, June 11, 2004, 4:20 p.m. "Peter, can I ask you a quick question?" I'm standing at the desk of one of my fellow copy editors because I don't want to bother Barry, my boss, when he's on deadline—especially on a day like today, with all the stories and photos coming in from the Reagan funeral.

Peter turns to me, so I go on: "This story's about a sanitation worker. What's the headline word for that?"

"Sanit man," he says in his cheery Australian accent. Peter is one of the many employees who came here to the *New York Post* after working for other papers owned by Australian media magnate Rupert Murdoch.

"Just 'sanit,' no point?" On the copy desk we say *point* instead of *period*. I'm not sure why, except perhaps that it takes less time to say. Everything here has to get done quickly.

"That's right," Peter answers.

"Thanks." I return to my cubicle a few feet away.

Looking again at the story's chit—a small piece of white paper that Barry handed me when he assigned me the story to copyedit—I check the numbers that Barry wrote on it with a fine-point red marker. They tell me how many column inches the story should be, along with the specifications for its headline's width, number of lines, and font size.

After a few tries, playing around a bit with the kerning and leading, I come up with a two-line hed: *Judge saves job of 'trauma' sanit man.* It's not great art, but there's no room to be witty with an article like this.

Must give it one last read to make sure I didn't miss anything. The lede is nice and concise: "A sanitation worker who went AWOL for five months last year has avoided firing by convincing a judge he was traumatized while on duty at Ground Zero."

As my eyes scan down to reread the rest of the story, I pause at the last line. It says the worker spent four months, seven days a week, cleaning up at the site where the World Trade Center had stood.

Seven days a week. God bless him. I didn't even set foot upon Ground Zero—I was only a Red Cross volunteer on a boat docked there, serving food to people like that sanitation man who had been out combing debris for remains of people's loved ones—and all I could take was a few hours before I had to get away.

It was exactly two weeks after the 9/11 attacks. Officials were still calling the work at Ground Zero a rescue operation even though it was obvious that there were no survivors left to be found.

The memory is etched in my mind. I can see myself spooning chicken nuggets to a black female police officer; to a young Latino man in military fatigues; to an older, Irish-looking man in an FDNY uniform. Each one has dust from the site on his or her clothes; some are nearly coated with it. They all look shell-shocked, yet they are all unfailingly polite. "Thank you . . ." they say. "Thank you . . ."

These brave, selfless people, I thought, have spent the day in a war zone. What happened to America was an act of war. But when I went home at the end of the day and switched on National Public Radio, I heard liberal pundits take pains to emphasize that Islam was "a religion of peace."

As a new Christian who took the Gospel literally, I was already sympathetic to political conservativism on social issues such as the right to life and the dignity of marriage. The Christians I met who were engaged in the pro-life movement struck me as genuinely warmhearted people, not the wild-eyed, bomb-throwing fanatics that popular media depictions had led me to envision.

But 9/11 pushed me over the edge. I wanted to be around political conservatives—people unafraid to discuss the dangers of radical Islam. With the help of friends, I found groups such as the Fabiani Society and the New York City Young Republicans that bring together people like me who don't fit in with this crazy left-wing city.

All of which is to say: *Lord, I'm grateful you lifted me out of joblessness and—with the help of a recommendation from my "Postie" friend Joshua—into a full-time position as a copy editor and headline writer at the* New York Post.

Not counting the *Wall Street Journal*, the *Post* is the city's most conservative daily newspaper, the only one that consistently supports our president and our men and women fighting in Iraq.

True, the tabloid is not as conservative as I would like. For instance, Murdoch likes its pages to be dotted with pictures of women in their underwear. But even so, until I can get a job at *National Review* or Morality in Media, this is the closest I can get to a job in New York City where I don't have to check my Christian faith at the door.

I am grateful, too, that I get paid not only to copyedit stories but also to write pun-laden headlines. Just this week I encapsulated in four words the confession of a man who murdered his fiancée's feline: "Cat killer's meow culpa."

There are still things missing from my life, things I ask of the Lord every day: a church that really feels like home and a husband who is a man after the Lord's heart. But at least for now I truly have a dream job, doing the kind of work that many people would pay to do. *Thank you, God.*

Eight minutes later. I have to calm down.

Drink a sip of water, take some deep breaths. Don't walk up to Barry's desk until I can speak rationally and dispassionately.

Dear Lord, please help me, because I really have to do something about this latest story Barry gave me to copyedit. I can't leave it the way it is. Just looking at it makes me mad.

One more sip of water. One more deep breath. Okay.

I pick up the chit, put my hands on my desk to push myself up from my chair, turn around, and walk about five steps over to Barry's cubicle.

Barry lifts his eyes from his computer screen and turns to me. "What's up?" he asks in a staccato burst. I can tell he means for me to speak quickly, as he's rushing to complete the bulldog edition.

I hand him the chit. Normally I only give a chit back when I've finished copyediting the article.

"Barry, I read this story but I haven't yet written the headline, because it seems to me that it's written in a way that might confuse readers. It says Nancy Reagan's calling for an expansion in 'controversial' stem-cell research on Alzheimer's." I flash two fingers with each hand to note the quotation marks around "controversial." "And it says that, in doing so, she's placing herself in opposition to Bush, who put limits on federal funding for stem-cell research."

"But," I go on breathlessly, as I know Barry wants me to wrap up, "it doesn't explain why the research is controversial. And it's confusing because there are different kinds of stem-cell research, and not all of them are controversial.

"Bush didn't place any limits on funding of adult stem-cell research. There's no controversy there. What he limited was funding for *embryonic* stem-cell research. And that's what Nancy Reagan wants to change; she wants those limits lifted. *That's* what's controversial."

"Oh!" Barry says. "I see what you're saying."

"Right now," I add, "as it stands, a reader picking up this story would think *all* stem-cell research was controversial. And that's not true."

"Okay," Barry says. "I'll let the national desk know and see what they say."

"Thanks. Anything else for me?"

"Not right now."

"Okay." Back to waiting. That's the rhythm of life here on the copy desk: my fellow copy editors and I wait leisurely until the stories arrive, and then we spring into action.

I look to my Australian comrade, who is relaxing while reading Tim Blair's blog. "Peter, can I have some of your Vegemite?"

"You're the only American I know who likes this stuff," Peter replies with a smile as he hands me the jar. "Remember, it tastes best if you spread it thinly."

"I know," I say as I take a plastic knife out of my drawer and, with my back to Peter, spread a thick glob of the greasy brown goo over the bread that came with my takeout salad.

After I give Peter back his Vegemite, I pull out my shoulder bag from beneath my desk. Might as well take care of some bills, since there's nothing else to do.

Here's the page I tore out from the American Chesterton Society's *Gilbert* magazine with the form I have to fill out to register for the G.K. Chesterton Pilgrimage. I have to decide today whether to send in my check so that I can make this ten-day trip to England.

Above the form is an ad for the pilgrimage. It says, "Although we will 'see the sights,' this adventure is designed to be more in the nature of a religious pilgrimage. In conjunction with our visits to places connected to G.K. Chesterton, there will be daily lectures, discussions, and readings."

It sounds really lovely. I've been wanting to return to England, especially London—it's my favorite place in the world—but I've been afraid to go by myself. There are too many ghosts there—memories of men I loved and of men who desired me in a way that made me feel special. Now that I'm waiting until marriage, I'm lonely enough without having to be reminded of all the things I can't do anymore.

I'll make the pilgrimage. It will be an expensive trip. But if it gives me a chance to re-experience England within an environment of Christian fellowship, it will be worth it.

And who knows? Maybe my future husband is looking at this same page from *Gilbert* magazine. Wouldn't that be exciting if God were to bring me together with him in England! And if he were a Christian who shared my love of Chesterton!

Sigh. If only. Probably I'll arrive in England and find that, apart from the society's president, Dale Ahlquist, it's just me and a bunch of retired women. But it will still be a chance to discover if there is anything I love about England that can be redeemed.

Sunday, August 8, 2004, 10:35 a.m. All right. I've seen enough of this dreary, dark church with its cold Byzantine art. The Mass is getting into full swing and I really don't feel like sticking around for yet another boring service that I can't really be part of. I need air.

Outside now and down the steps. That's better.

The sun has yet to come out from behind the clouds. At least it's not raining. The neighborhood is unfamiliar but I have my *London A to Z* in my purse in case I get lost.

Why did we have to go to Westminster *Cathedral*? If we're going to go to a Westminster something-or-other, why couldn't it at least be Westminster *Abbey*, where all those famous people are buried? I know it's not Catholic, but it used to be.

It is now nine days since I arrived in England for the Chesterton pilgrimage. I still can't believe how naïve I was to assume it would be anything other than a celebration of Catholicism—or that there would be any other non-Catholics on the bus.

Although the tour has included Chesterton's former home, the makeshift Chesterton museum at Oxford, and a few other places relevant to his life, the vast majority of it has been visits to this church and that church, all of which are "ours" or "used to be ours."

Every day the bus stops at a church for daily Mass. And I went along every day but today, reading my book of Psalms while the others went up for Communion. Dale mentioned to me that I could go up for a blessing if I wanted, so I tried that once. It was okay.

I also tried to read the Psalms while the rest of the pilgrims recited the rosary each day on the bus. But between daily Mass and daily rosary, I went through all 150 of David's hymns in a week. So, as of yesterday, I decided instead to use the rosary time to read the newspaper and reapply my lipstick.

It looks now like it's going to rain at any moment. Good thing for me that there's so much construction in this neighborhood; the scaffolding may be unattractive but it will afford protection in a downpour. I knew I shouldn't have left my umbrella on the bus.

Feeling so lonely. I thought I would have Christian fellowship on this pilgrimage. Instead it's been isolating.

I shouldn't feel sorry for myself. It's wrong. My tourmates are sweet, kind, friendly people.

But I can't help it. I do feel lonely.

When I accepted Jesus, I thought that I would never again have to endure having a Christian lecture me on what I had to do to be saved. But practically every day on this trip a different person has taken me aside to try to win me over to Rome.

They try to do it in a friendly way. An Englishman who is helping lead the pilgrimage asked me kindly to tell him what was preventing me from becoming Catholic.

I didn't feel like giving him the whole list of things the Catholic Church says or does that are unbiblical, so I focused on Mary. There's nothing in the Bible, I said, about praying to her or to anyone other than God.

Then, as happens so often in these conversations, my friendly conversation partner became a well-meaning but aggressive apologist. He first brought me to admit that I ask friends to pray for me. Yes, I said, seeing where he was going, but my friends aren't dead.

Well, he replied, isn't Mary in heaven? And wouldn't her prayers be more valuable because she is praying them in heaven rather than on earth?

But then it really makes no sense to pray to her, I said. If I am going to pray to someone in heaven, why not pray to God?

Then my antagonist changed tactics to focus on Mary's relationship to Jesus. "If you want something from your boss," he said, "you ask the boss's mother."

As I hear those words in my memory, I shudder in disgust. Is that what Catholics really believe? That the saints, even Jesus' mother, are some kind of favor bank in the sky? And that Jesus hears and answers prayers not according to his boundless love but rather according to nepotism? That the life of heaven imitates the sinfulness of earthly life, where one has to play politics to gain the boss's ear? If that's the true Catholic faith, then I want no part of it.

And that's not even what irks me most about my fellow pilgrims' efforts to convert me. The award for that goes to the tactic that several pilgrims have attempted, each unaware that others have already tried it and failed. They say, "You're Jewish! Have you ever heard of Edith Stein?"

As if the one thing that could convince me to become Catholic would be if I knew of a Jewish woman, someone *just like me*—not!—who converted and became a saint. As if I were simply a Jew who wanted to do whatever other Jews do, rather than someone who seeks the truth and cleaves to it. As if my baptism made no difference at all. As if I were on the road to perdition, whatever perdition is.

I'm not going to think about it. It just makes me mad, and I don't want to be mad. It's Sunday.

Walking faster now. There's the Apollo Victoria Theatre, with its huge orange-and-black sign advertising a stage version of *Saturday Night Fever*. Good thing I no longer depend on being a Sixties rock historian for income; pop culture has moved on to nostalgia for the decade of my childhood. Unbelievable. I'm only thirty-five and already I'm an oldie.

Check my watch; it's 10:50 already. I must have about thirty minutes more before the end of Mass. Must walk faster if I want to see more of the London streets, the streets I used to walk in search of vinyl records, vintage clothes, books, rock magazines, and the man I never found, the man who would love me.

Self-pity again. It's a repeat of how I felt at this time yesterday, when the bus drove into London. I had hoped we would visit the houses where Chesterton and his wife lived when they were young, or the school where he studied art, or the Fleet Street buildings where the newspapers he wrote for were based. But all I saw of Fleet Street was through the bus's windows, and instead of stopping at Chesterton's house, we stopped at the home of some nuns.

The convent was called Tyburn and the pilgrims were excited because it was known to have a chapel filled with relics of the English martyrs. I had no desire to look at a collection of bones, so I opted to take a walk around as I am doing now. Except that there was nothing really to see except Hyde Park across the street, and I knew that walking around the green space would only make me wish I had a special man who would enjoy it with me.

So, after a walk around the block, I found myself on the steps of Tyburn with only my pocket Gideons New Testament/Psalms/Proverbs and my digital camera for company. And, as I sat down, a wave of loneliness hit me suddenly. I had that choked-up feeling that I used to get when I was suicidal. It was scary.

I managed to distract myself by taking some self-portraits with my camera. It was interesting to see how my face looked drained of both color and joy. Then I just talked to God for a while, telling him how awful I felt. And I wished I'd taken my full Bible off the bus, as I really needed to re-read that passage from Jeremiah 29 about how God knows the plans he has for me.

That was yesterday. I thought I was past that loneliness. And now here I am, weaving my way briskly through the tourist-clogged sidewalks along Wilton Road, still with that same old feeling.

Dear God, I feel so sad. I don't want to feel sad, Lord. Please help me.

I'm not at church, Lord. I feel like I should be. At least, I should be somewhere with people who are praying on a Sunday. Please help me. Please help me find a place where I fit in. Please help me find a community that feels like home. Please send me the right man, in your time, Lord, according to your will.

I pause my prayer. It feels like a moment to be quiet and take in the experience of being lonely in London.

A feeling comes up inside me that I don't understand. It hurts but I feel somehow that it is better for me to hurt than not to feel the pain.

God is walking with me.

How can that be? If I really felt him with me, then I wouldn't feel so lonely.

But he is with me. He just is.

10 Yesterday's Papers

Monday, January 17, 2005, 8:30 p.m. I'm doomed. I messed up big time. And there is nothing I can do but sit here in my cubicle at the *Post* and wait for the axe to fall, as it inevitably will.

If only I could turn back the clock to two Saturdays ago, January 8, when Milt, the deputy copy chief, gave me the chit to Susan Edelman's story. If only. But what would I have done differently?

I would have given Milt the chit back and asked for a different story. And I would have risked getting fired for refusing to do the work I was assigned. But at least then I would have done nothing wrong—nothing against God's law, anyway. It would only have been a case of conscientious objection. That's not a sin.

But instead I looked at the story about a doctor who was using in vitro fertilization to enable women with uterine cancer to have one last chance of getting pregnant prior to their hysterectomies, and I got mad. Really mad.

The reporter wanted to convey a tale of brave women risking everything for biological motherhood. But what I saw in the story was something more complex and disturbing. To me, the cancer-stricken would-be moms were being exploited by a doctor who not only was putting their own lives in danger but also was disregarding the very humanity of their embryonic children.

What sparked my fury was the line that said that, after a woman had three embryos implanted, "two took." The story then swept into an account of the courage of this woman who was about to give birth to twins, with no mention of the fact that one child died to make the two surviving babies.

By then I had read enough about IVF to know it was a crapshoot. The IVF process required doctors to produce "surplus" embryos for each patient; the extras were required in case a particular embryo failed to implant. Since each of those embryos was an unborn child whose life had dignity, thousands upon thousands of human beings were being scientifically manufactured to be "spares." It was almost akin to creating people for the sake of destroying them.

The story hit me especially hard because of my obsession with pro-life issues, a change that has come over me only recently.

It started when I did some digging on the internet—Barry lets copy editors web-surf while awaiting stories—and found that Planned Parenthood's Teenwire website encourages children as young as six to register to ask questions of "sexperts." The site's main content consists of interactive games, quizzes, and how-to essays instructing kids on topics such as how to troll for homosexual sex partners online and how heterosexual couples can "use anal sex as a way to preserve the woman's virginity." It also features a link to another website, Scarleteen, where children can purchase pornography and sadomasochistic sex toys without being asked their age.

I can't describe how angry it made me to discover those websites and learn how Planned Parenthood and its allies were exposing children to adult sexual perversions. Until I found those sites, I thought perhaps I could be a Christian without being one of those crazy pro-life campaigners. No more. Now, whatever Planned Parenthood is for, I have to be against. It is an evil organization and it must be stopped. I do my part by posting on my blog, *The Dawn Patrol*, nearly every day about the latest insane thing I found on Teenwire or some other Planned Parenthood website.

The anger I felt over Planned Parenthood and the mentality that treats children, whether born or unborn, as objects to be subjected to adults' whims—it all came to the surface when I was reading that stupid IVF story. I stared at those words, "two took," and thought about all the babies languishing in orphanages and foster homes because they had handicaps like Down syndrome and no one wanted them. I thought about the black babies given up by poor mothers who were raised by the state because there weren't enough black couples who wanted to adopt them, and most white couples only wanted white babies. All those babies—*born* babies—lacked loving homes while IVF doctors raked in large salaries by playing Russian roulette with the unborn. It was capitalism at its most selfish—doctors trafficking in human lives.

So I took matters into my own hands. Before the words "two took," I added some words of my own: "One died." And I added some educational information elsewhere in the story, saying that in the process of IVF, embryos were routinely destroyed.

I tried to make the changes in a way that wouldn't be too obvious, because I didn't want to get caught. But as soon as I turned in the story, I knew that I would get caught and there would be hell to pay. And now there is.

The story didn't make the cut for the Sunday paper, so it was held until this past Sunday, the fifteenth. Only two readers noticed that anything about it was off. Unfortunately for me those two readers were the IVF doctor and the author. And Susan won't be satisfied until she has my head on a platter.

I found out about the reaction yesterday when Barry called while I was home sick with a sinus infection. He told me that the editors went ballistic. The only way he managed to keep them from forcing him to fire me was by pointing out to them that I'd never done anything like that in my three years on the job.

Barry told me I had to promise him I'd never make such changes to a story again. I promised. He also said the editor-in-chief of the paper also insisted I write a letter of apology to Susan, so I emailed her right away.

Any hopes I had that Susan might accept my apology were dashed when I saw the header of her reply. It was just one word, all-caps: SABOTAGE.

Today I showed up for work as usual, but it's been five and a half hours and Barry has only given me one story to copyedit. I can feel the tension all around me in the newsroom. It has started to hit me that, however much Barry would like to keep me, there is no way his bosses are going to let me remain here.

I have failed everybody.

I failed my employer and my colleagues, especially Barry. He believed in me to the point of risking his own reputation to save me.

I failed the pro-life movement by perpetuating the myth that pro-lifers are unscrupulous. Now it will be harder than ever for someone like me to get a job at the *Post*.

Worst of all, I failed God. Ephesians 6 says I should serve my employer as I would serve the Lord. It would be wrong to try to deceive God. What I did was a sin.

Then there's the fact that I have destroyed any chances that a New York City newspaper or magazine will ever hire me again.

What is left for me? Begging rock-magazine editors for assignments and trying to get interviews at temp agencies? Again? At the age of thirty-six?

Perhaps some Christian nonprofit might hire me? It's not likely. First of all, I'd probably have to move to some place well outside New York City where there actually are fervent Christians in large numbers. And then, why would a Christian employer want someone whose main experience is as a rock historian? Nonprofits want college-age interns, not seasoned journalists. Yesterday I called my one connection in that world, Patrick at Morality in Media, to ask if he knew of any opportunities for someone with my experience and abilities. He didn't.

I wish . . . I wish . . .

I wish I had a friend in heaven. Someone who would understand what I'm going through.

That's silly. Jesus is my friend in heaven.

Yes. But still . . . I wish I had a friend in heaven who understood what I am going through.

Jesus knows what it's like to be cursed by a mob. But he doesn't know what it's like to incur the wrath of the *New York Post*. At least, he doesn't know how it feels to go through this experience knowing that, even if I don't deserve to be fired, I am guilty just the same. He may have perfect sympathy for me, but he only knows what it's like to suffer as an innocent person, not what it's like when you realize you messed up.

When I talked to Patrick yesterday, I asked him a question I never thought I'd ask anyone: whether there was a patron saint of journalists. I'm that desperate.

It still feels wrong to send up prayers to anyone other than God. But I'm already on God's bad side. Could asking a saint's help make it worse? My Catholic friends are good people. I can't imagine they're going to hell because they asked St. Francis to help them find their lost dog or something.

Maybe, in God's plan, he permits people to ask saints for help. Why would he? I don't know. And I don't want to make a habit of it. But if good people are doing it and they say it gets results, I'll try it just this once.

Patrick said St. Francis de Sales is the patron of journalists. But he didn't tell me anything else about the saint, and I didn't question him further for fear of opening up a door for him to try to convert me. So I'll type "Francis de Sales" into Google and see if anything about his life comes up that would make me want to ask him for help . . .

Well, that's disappointing. All I can find is that de Sales was a bishop in Switzerland who wrote pamphlets. Why would the Catholic Church make someone a patron of journalists who never worked at a newspaper?

Maybe I'll have better luck if I put the words *patron saint journalists* into Google.

The first result is a page from an index of saints for every occasion. Two are listed as patrons of journalists: de Sales and Maximilian Kolbe. But Maximilian is also listed as a patron saint of pro-lifers! Now we're getting somewhere!

I Google some more and find an online biography of St. Maximilian on a site called catholic-pages.com. It says his birthday is January 8—one day after Curt Boettcher's, and the same day as David Bowie and Elvis Presley. I like him already.

The biography is a long read, but that's all right; it's not like I have anything else to do right now but worry.

It says St. Maximilian was a Franciscan friar in Poland during the first part of the twentieth century. But what does that have to do with journalism? Oh, I see . . . he ran a publishing operation out of his friary, including a daily newspaper that had a Sunday circulation of 225,000. Wow! When the Germans invaded, he opened up the friary to Polish refugees, including 2,000 Jews . . .

A saint who sheltered Jews. I can hardly believe it.

Tears are coming out. I pick up my purse from the floor and pull out a tissue—darn, it's my last one—and wipe my face, glancing around to make sure no one sees.

A patron saint of journalists and pro-lifers who cared for Jews. Perhaps St. Maximilian will care for me too.

Back to the bio. It says the Nazis came for him after he published these words:

> No one in the world can change Truth. What we can do and should do is to seek truth and to serve it when we have found it. The real conflict is the inner conflict. Beyond armies of occupation and the hecatombs of extermination camps, there are two irreconcilable enemies in the depth of every soul: good and evil, sin and love. And what use are the victories on the battlefield if we ourselves are defeated in our innermost personal selves?

They sent him to Auschwitz. I am stunned. Had no idea any Catholics were sent there, let alone priests.

The bio tells about Fr. Kolbe's selfless generosity to his fellow prisoners and how he retained his humanity even as he was singled out for beatings by a guard.

I am entranced as I read. St. Maximilian seems alive to me. He writes to his mother from the camp: "Do not worry about me or my health, for the good Lord is everywhere and holds every one of us in his great love."

Now the article moves on to the "last act" in St. Maximilian's life. I'd better steel myself.

This part of the story is told through first-person testimonies of eyewitnesses. I've never seen that in a saint's biography before; usually it is just writings from some person who writes in flowery language about how holy the saint was. This is different. This is real.

After three prisoners escaped, the SS officers rounded up the prisoners in Kolbe's cell block. The senior officer announced that, as punishment for the escape, they would select ten men whom they would send to an underground bunker to die of starvation.

One of the men who was picked was a former Polish soldier. When the guard called out his number and told him to come away, he cried out, "Oh, my poor wife, my poor children. I shall never see them again."

Then Fr. Kolbe stepped out from the ranks and spoke to the head SS officer. He asked to change places with the distraught man. And, miraculously, the officer let him.

Tears again. I hastily open my cubicle's top drawer and grab a couple of takeout napkins.

Even in the starvation cell, St. Maximilian encouraged the other prisoners, leading them in prayers and song. An eyewitness who assisted the janitor in the bunker says that when he heard them, he had the impression he was in a church.

Kolbe kept up the spirits of his fellow prisoners for two weeks, until he was the only one left. Finally the Nazis sent someone in to give him a shot of carbolic acid. Here again, remarkably, there is a quote from an eyewitness: "Fr. Kolbe, with a prayer on his lips, himself gave his arm to the executioner."

What an amazing man. I have to read more about him. Putting his name into Google again, I find another biography of the saint on Kolbenet.com. It has a more vivid description of his final moments. At the bottom, it adds, "The man whose place Fr. Kolbe took was present for the beatification of Blessed Kolbe, a confessor, by Pope Paul VI on October 17, 1971. On October 10, 1982, Pope John Paul II canonized him Saint Maximilian Maria Kolbe, a martyr."

As I read those words, I can see Gajowniczek in St. Peter's Square. I think about how he lived for decades after Kolbe saved his life. I imagine what it must have been like for him to witness the pope declare Kolbe one of the holy ones of God.

My heart explodes.

One more glance around; no one is looking. Another takeout napkin to my face.

Under my breath, I say, *Dear St. Maximilian, I'm in trouble. I'm about to be fired. Please help me.*

Even as the words "please help me" come out, I can feel that something is different. The tears are flowing again but the tears feel different. Something deep inside me changed, immediately, as I prayed those words.

There is no doubt in my mind that St. Maximilian, up in heaven, is sending me love. He is praying that I may know the peace of God, the peace that surpasses all understanding.

It doesn't make sense. There is no reason why I should feel peace right now. I did everything wrong, I am about to be fired, it feels like I have no future . . .

Yet I *do* feel peace, amid these tears that are now tears of joy. I feel as though I had strayed somewhere far off the map, and God, through St. Maximilian's prayers, picked me up and planted me exactly where he wants me to be.

I don't deserve this mercy. I don't deserve this love. I don't deserve this strange and sudden calm, as though I were in the eye in the midst of the storm.

But I have it. It is a feeling of joy. I recognize this feeling from when I experienced it during the first few days after my conversion. I felt it again from my baptism. It must be the Holy Spirit.

No matter what happens to me now, everything will be okay.

I don't know how I know that. It doesn't even make sense. I just know.

About six hours later. Winding down now for the evening, or rather morning. Too sleepy to read any more from the Bible.

I check to make sure the space heater is away from the stacks of papers on my floor, switch off the light and slip into bed, turning toward the alarm to make sure it is set.

Dear God, thank you so much for St. Maximilian. Thank you for answering my prayer.

Lord, I am probably going to be fired tomorrow—I mean, today. I may even have to meet with the editor-in-chief, Col Allan. Please, Lord, whatever happens, please don't let me cry. I don't want to cry because the editors already think I'm crazy and that will just confirm it for them. Please let me be strong. Dear St. Maximilian, please pray that I won't cry and that I will be strong. I pray this in Jesus' name, amen.

Tuesday, January 18, 2005, 5:37 p.m.
Everybody in this cramped side office is tense. *New York*

Post office manager Annie, who faces me from behind the desk, is tense. Barry, seated to my left by the glass wall that separates us from the newsroom, is tense. And I am tense.

In Barry's hand is a copy of a letter he gave me yesterday that describes how I made unauthorized changes to Susan's story. I am to sign the letter on the understanding that it will remain in my file, and if I do anything wrong from this point on, I will be fired.

Given that I have admitted what I did wrong, apologized to Susan and the editors, and agreed to be on probation for the rest of my time at the *Post*, it would seem that, once I sign the letter, there would be closure on the situation. Susan's still not likely to want to be my best friend anytime soon, but there is nothing more I can do to make things right.

But what I'm gathering from Barry right now is that what really concerns the editors, all the way up to Col Allan, has nothing to do with my job performance. It's the *Dawn Patrol*. Barry explains that the editors have made printouts of my blog—he lifts up a pile of papers from his lap—and they are scanning them for references to the *Post*, which are not hard to find since I do write about my personal life.

"But the *Post* doesn't have a policy on employees' blogging," I protest.

"I'm aware of that," Barry says. He seems exasperated, not with me but rather with the idea that his bosses would go to such lengths to find evidence to use against me.

Barry adds that what most disturbed Col was that I posted a blog entry during work time yesterday.

Hmm. Was Col angry only because I posted a blog entry while at work, or did the entry itself inflame him? I wrote about a pro-life blog that is sponsoring an art contest for depictions of the time when Planned Parenthood founder Margaret Sanger spoke at a Ku Klux Klan rally.

In any case, I have to defend myself. "But when I first started on the copy desk, you told me that during down time I was free to use the internet, send emails, make phone calls . . ."

"That's right, I did," Barry says. Looking at Annie, he adds, "Dawn's using the internet has never been a problem on the job. It *is* a problem for some people on the desk: I'll give them an assignment and, five minutes later, I'll see them on the internet and I'll have to tell them to get to work. But it's never a problem with Dawn. Whenever I give her an assignment, she drops whatever she's doing to work on it."

"But," Annie replies, "she does work on personal projects while on the job."

Barry shrugs. "That's true. Technically, no one on the copy desk is supposed to do any personal work. But everyone does."

He turns to look at me, making eye contact. His expression is grave and earnest.

"So, Dawn, I realize—and I explained this to Col—that you were never warned against blogging during your shift. But from now on, you've gotta be extra careful. I can't emphasize it enough."

"I will. I promise. I'm so sorry, Barry."

"All right. Good."

Annie has been watching us with hands folded. "All right," she says, addressing both of us. "Are you ready to sign and initial the letter?"

Right at that moment, the phone on Annie's desk rings and she picks up. I have a bad feeling about this.

My intuition was correct. It was Col and he wants to see Barry right away. Barry exits; I stay to sign and initial the letter.

No sooner do I lift up my pen from the letter than the phone rings again. It's Col; this time he wants to meet with me.

Dear St. Maximilian, help me. Pray for me.

I know what's coming. No doubt Annie does too. She leads me into Col's office. It's a large rectangle that runs halfway across the far end of the newsroom. This office too has a glass wall; through it the editor can keep an eye on the entire newsroom if he wishes.

Never in my three years of working for the *Post* has Col ever spoken to me, let alone had me enter his office. All I've heard are stories about his brusque leadership style and his close working relationship with Murdoch, who brought him here from his native Australia. I think of him as an extension of Murdoch.

Now I see him seated at his large cherry-wood desk, looking at some papers; I can guess they're printouts of my blog. It's obvious he's not happy.

He doesn't bother to shake my hand. As I take a seat, I can see through the window that Barry has returned to the copy desk. Annie lingers in the back of the office.

There is a moment of silence as Col looks at one of the papers. Finally he lifts up his head.

"I was *stunned*," he says in a rough-edged Australian staccato.

"I was stunned," he repeats, "to hear what you did to Susan Edelman's article. Why did you make those changes?"

I take a deep breath. "I could tell you what was in my head at the time I made them, but I now realize that it was wrong. There are times, as a copy editor, when an important piece of information may be missing from a story and it's my job to put it in. But I should never have inserted information on something that was controversial. The controversial nature of the subject should have raised a red flag for me. I'm very sorry about what I did."

Col glares at me. "Do you know what you did? By inserting that information, you put your own opinion—your own *spin*—into that story."

I nod silently, trying to look respectful. I've already said I'm sorry. On one level, he's right about the spin. But even if I was wrong to make the change, what I wrote was true.

"When the editors told me what you did, I was ready to fire you. But Barry insisted to me that you were a good copy editor and you were needed. So I agreed to let you stay.

"But then they told me about these," Col continues, holding up printouts of the *Dawn Patrol*. "I'm very disturbed about your blog."

My eyes widen. I don't know how to respond to that.

"You wrote that a story we published was wrong."

Now I have to say something. "I've never done that."

Col begins to read from the top printout. I recognize the blog entry; I wrote it last Sunday morning about a *Post* story for which I wrote the front-page headline "JERSEY JIHAD."

The *Post* article claimed that the as-yet-unsolved slaying of a Jersey City Coptic Christian family might have been in retaliation for anti-Muslim remarks made online. I noted that the *New York Times*, in reporting on the same story, was more cautious about a possible motive in the killings.

What angered Col were my closing words. It's strange to hear him read my words out loud: "It could be that the assertions the *Post* story makes are false."

I want to jump in and say that my wording was clumsy. I didn't intend to doubt the *Post*'s reporting, only to hesitate before accepting the words of its sources who were quick to blame Muslims for the crime. My point was, whether or not the attack was, as the reporter insinuated, a Jersey jihad, we as a country needed to get serious about fighting terror and hatred.

But before I can defend myself, Col moves on. "So I am firing you, and the reason I am firing you is because, even after Barry spoke to you about what you did to Susan's story, and you knew you were on notice, you wrote a blog entry during work time."

So this is really about my blog entry on the Margaret Sanger Ku Klux Klan rally art contest.

Now I can't be silent. I pour out all the defenses I made in Annie's office—Barry encouraged me to use the internet, it never interfered with my work . . .

"None of that matters," Col replies, "because you had the nerve to blog on company time after you were told that any further infractions would result in your being fired."

My heart races. Must stay calm.

For the good of Col's soul, I have to warn him about what he is doing. It would be one thing if he were firing me for what I did to Susan's story. But if he's firing me for blogging against Planned Parenthood—which he must be, as it's well known that I'm far from the only *Post* employee who blogs on company time—then I must fraternally correct him. But how to do it without its sounding like a threat?

Another deep breath. "Sir," I say—for he hasn't said I could call him by his name—"you're older than I am, and you've been in this business for much longer than I have. And I'm sure that from where you're sitting, you're making the right decision.

"But from where I'm sitting, it's the *wrong* decision."

Col's face reddens. He leans over to put his palms on his desk, pushing himself up into a standing position. Then he lifts his right arm to point at me accusingly as he shouts:

"YOU ARE A LIABILITY!"

I hightail it out of Col's door; Annie follows and leads me back to her office, where Barry rejoins us.

Barry is crushed when Annie tells him I was fired. "Dawn, I'm so sorry for the way this whole thing was conducted. You've been on a roller coaster."

"It's all right, Barry. You did everything you could for me. I really appreciate it."

Annie can't answer my questions about severance pay and whether the *Post* would contest my unemployment benefits; she says for me to call her tomorrow. For now, she can only give me a cardboard box for the contents of my desk, plus a voucher for a hired car to take me and my belongings back to Hoboken.

Since Col made it clear that I am *persona non grata* here, I'd better not try to say goodbye to my colleagues. They all know why I am packing my things.

It is absolutely miraculous that I have not yet cried.

William, one of the quieter members of the copy desk, approaches me as I load up my box. "Dawn, I'm sorry . . ."

I look up and see that William's arms are extended to hug me. Now I am crying.

Once I finish packing, Barry chivalrously picks up my box to walk me out to the hired car. But I am only a few steps beyond what was my cubicle when I realize I forgot to do something.

Barry had earlier asked everyone on the copy desk to think about a headline for Sunday's front page. Donald Trump, the relentlessly self-promoting real-estate mogul and star of *The Apprentice*, is getting married again and the front page is to feature a photo of the bride in her dress. I have an idea and I need to give it to Milt, our deputy copy chief who does the Sunday paper, while it's still in my mind.

"Milt!" I shout so he can hear me; he's fifteen feet away. "For Sunday! 'The Lady Is a Trump!'"

"Good one, Dawn!" Milt smiles. "Thanks!"

Barry walks with me out of the newsroom to the elevator bank. "I'm so sorry, Dawn. I'm sorry to lose you."

"Thanks, Barry. I'm sorry to go."

"I can't believe Annie couldn't answer your questions about unemployment and severance pay. That's unheard of. Even when the 'massacre' happened, with six people fired in one day, the HR people were notified beforehand."

"It's okay, Barry," I reply as the elevator doors close and we travel down to the lobby.

"I'm really sorry about this, I feel so bad about what you had to go through . . ."

"Really, Barry, I'll be fine. Don't worry about me. God is taking care of me."

Wednesday, January 19, 2005, 7:31 p.m. I peer down the dimly lit bar at the fifty or so people who have come here to Sláinte, this cozy Irish bar on the Bowery. It's a familiar and yet unfamiliar sight.

The sight is familiar because, save for a few newcomers, it's the same crowd I've seen here ever since my *Post* colleague Mark and I had the idea of starting the Manhattan Project, a monthly social for that rarest of rare breeds: conservatives in the NYC media. But it's unfamiliar because I can no longer socialize with them from the elevated standpoint of a full-time *Post* employee. Now I am just another unemployed blogger struggling to find work.

I haven't yet told my *Dawn Patrol* readers about losing my job. About twelve hundred readers visit the blog each day to read my latest exposés of the abortion industry and I don't want to have to answer their questions while my energies are taken up with job-hunting. My family and friends know, and everyone else will soon enough—especially given how quickly rumors travel in the media business.

An unfamiliar man holding a bottle of beer approaches me. "Excuse me, are you Dawn Eden?" His slight twang marks him as a Midwesterner.

I try to make out his features in the shadows. He is about my age, medium height, clean shaven, and looks to have a friendly face; yes, he is handsome. This is great. It feels like it's been ages since a handsome man has approached me in a bar, or anywhere for that matter.

"Yes."

"I'm George Gurley from the *New York Observer.*"

George Gurley! A friend told me Gurley was trying to reach me. I had no idea why. He writes about celebrities and socialites.

"Nice to meet you!"

"Uh, thanks," he says, a bit nervously. "I was wondering if I might interview you sometime. I'd like to do a story about your being a Christian working at the *New York Post.*"

Just my luck. I've dreamed of telling the world how I went from being a freewheeling rock journalist to a conservative Christian. Finally, someone from a major media publication wants to write about me, only now that he's tracked me down, I'm unable to satisfy the angle he's looking for. Darn.

"Well," I say, forcing a laugh, "I'm afraid I can't help you, unless you want to write about a Christian who just got fired from the *New York Post.*"

"Really! Wow! What happened?"

I take a sip of my grapefruit-and-seltzer. "I made a pro-life change to a pro-choice story. Col Allan wasn't very happy about that. Then, when I apologized, the editors showed him my blog. And he fired me over that."

"Awesome! Can I write about that?"

If George can see my face in this light, my surprise and joy must be visible. "You really want to?"

"It's an even better story!"

11 Homeward Bound

Monday, February 14, 2005, 11:30 a.m. I can hardly believe how much my situation has changed in just three weeks. Late last month I saw a therapist for help overcoming a black depression that overcame me as the reality of my firing sunk in.

My need for psychological help shocked me. Ever since my conversion, I had assumed God's grace would protect me from sliding back into nihilism. There were times during the past five years when I felt stressed out or sad, but always with an underlying sense of hope.

This time, that buffer was gone. For several days my thoughts were taken up with guilt, fear, and a kind of spiritual exhaustion. Although I managed just barely to fight off temptations to self-harm, it was scary.

As I emerged from my blue funk, George Gurley provided a needed distraction. A friend in the know told me I could trust him—he wrote warmly of Ann Coulter, and my views aren't nearly as controversial as hers—so I gave him all the details about what happened at the *Post*. But he turned out to be interested in more than that—he wanted to know about my whole life. We spent hours together in restaurants, bars, nightclubs—even the Strand bookstore, where he asked me to point out my favorite books.

It was exciting to be an object of interest for George. But it also made me lonely.

I found him attractive from the start, only he had a girlfriend; besides, it wouldn't have been right for him to have more than a professional relationship with me. The real challenge for me was that his research required him to observe me in various social situations and ask me intimate questions about my inner life.

It was as though for a week and a half I had the chaste boyfriend of my dreams, who found everything about me fascinating. Then, once he had all the information he needed, he turned in his story and moved on.

There's no doubt in my mind that George genuinely appreciates me. I'm more than a laboratory specimen to him. But when his research was done, he could return to a full life. For me, with no job and no boyfriend, when George said goodbye after his last time trailing me around Greenwich Village, I felt like a little kid when the circus leaves town.

Then the *Observer* hit newsstands last Wednesday with George's story right on the front page. Since then, I haven't had any time to feel lonely; my phone has not stopped ringing.

The story's headline plays up the sensational news that there exists some human being, somewhere, who is more conservative than Murdoch: "Eden in Exile: Chipper, Canned Headline Genius is Right of Rupert." But the accompanying photo, rather than depicting what many New

York City liberals think of when they imagine a female conservative—an uptight, grim-faced matron—shows me beaming while curled up shoeless on a couch, modeling the chicest outfit I own: a magenta mock-turtleneck, a white micro-miniskirt made of Chanel-style quilted vinyl, and mock-Pucci psychedelic tights.

George's article is written in Tom Wolfe's New Journalism style. But unlike Wolfe, George puts himself in the story. Although it's centered on my firing, its narrative arc includes his introducing himself to me, finding me fascinating, and meeting up with me at various places. My life story comes out through snippets of our conversations. He paints a verbal picture of how I look and even how I speak—with "a slight, adorable stutter." The result is that, whether or not readers warm to me personally as George does, he succeeds in depicting me as a true New York City character. Overnight I have become "interesting."

The most amazing result of my newfound fame was an email that arrived in my inbox the day that the *Observer* went on sale, inviting me to meet with the top editors of the *Daily News*—the *Post*'s competitor in Manhattan's tabloid wars. They actually want to discuss with me the possibility of joining their team.

I still can't believe it. The *News*, although moderate by New York City standards, is politically to the left of the *Post*. When I was fired, I couldn't imagine applying for a job there; it was so unlikely that they would hire me after what I did.

But the *News*'s editors told me they loved the pun-laden headlines of mine that Gurley cited in his article. So it looks like their desire to become more competitive with the *Post* outweighs any hesitance they might have had about my personal views. Maybe they also figure I've learned my lesson.

In any case, there is now a real possibility I might gain a position there.

That's not all. Popular websites like Gawker, National Review Online, and Arts & Letters Daily picked up the *Observer* story, bringing it to a national audience. That in turn led Christian book publishers to contact me—no fewer than four publishers in as many days.

The sudden interest was terrifically exciting, but it also baffled me. I asked one of the publishers why getting fired from the *Post* made me a hot property. He explained that my background in mainstream media, not to mention rock journalism, made me unusual among Christian writers.

Now I am waiting by the phone for a call from the publisher I would most like to sign with: Thomas Nelson, the largest Christian publisher in the United States. Acquisitions editor Greg Daniel and I had a great conversation last week and he asked me to come up with ideas. I have one idea that I think is highly marketable, and I could write it the way I normally write my blog, by taking outside sources and commenting upon them. That's not so hard for a former rock critic.

If Greg doesn't like my first idea, I do have a second one. But he probably won't like it, because nothing like it has ever been done. Also, it would require me to write the entire book out of my own head—in other words, to be an actual author.

The phone rings; I answer a bit breathlessly. Greg and I exchange pleasantries. Then the question comes: "Have you thought of any ideas for the book you'd like to write?"

"Yes, I have," I say, my voice gaining confidence and excitement with every word. "I'd like to write a book of pro-life answers to pro-choice questions."

Silence. If I didn't live in a city, I would be able to hear crickets right now.

Finally, Greg responds with the seasoned cheeriness of someone whose professional life is taken up with handling authors: "Do you have any other ideas?"

I pause briefly to gather my courage. Hope my stammer really does sound adorable, because Greg is going to get it whether he likes it or not.

"Well, um, there is something else I've been thinking about. You know, since I accepted Jesus, I've been trying to learn chastity, and I've been writing on my blog about what it's like to try to become chaste for someone who is, um, in her thirties and hasn't lived that way. And people seem—they seem to enjoy what I'm writing on that topic, and, um, there—there really isn't any book out there for adults on changing their lives in that area. There are books for teens on abstinence 'til marriage, but there, um, there doesn't seem to be anything for grown-ups like myself who, um, missed the bus as far as abstinence is concerned."

"That sounds great! Why don't you write a proposal and I'll run it past our acquisitions team?"

"Sure! I'd be delighted." Not. I mean, yes, I would be delighted to be an author, but not delighted to have to write a book out of my own head, and even less to tell the most intimate details of my struggle to grow in virtue. Can't I skip the part about writing the book and just become an author?

Oh, what am I thinking? This is awesome! *Thank you, God!*

Monday, June 20, 2005, 2:14 p.m. The phone rings in my cubicle in the *Daily News* newsroom. "Hello?"

It's a man with an Eastern European accent. "Hello, is this Dawn Eden?"

"Yes, this is Dawn!" My voice is friendlier that it would normally be for a stranger. I think I know who this is.

"This is Fr. Buda. You left me a message . . ."

"Yes, that's right!"

Finally, a priest who actually responds to my inquiry—within an hour of my voicemail message, no less!

I've been wanting to enter RCIA—the program for adults wishing to become Catholic—since shortly after my firing from the *Post*. Certainly St. Maximilian Kolbe's intercession played the greatest part in winning me over. It helped me to see that the Catholic understanding of the communion of saints wasn't idolatry; God really wants to grow in relationship with us by bringing us into relationship with those who live with him in heaven.

What solidified my decision was the experience of being persecuted for being pro-life. It struck me that Catholics had been persecuted for being pro-life for 2,000 years, and that my experience put me in solidarity with them.

Granted, I had Protestant friends who were pro-life, but their worship communities could change their understanding of the dignity of the child in the womb and still go on. But it seemed to me that the dignity of every human life, from conception to natural death, was inscribed into the Catholic Church's very identity. Even if individual bishops or organizations of Catholics failed to pass on pro-life teaching as they should, it was impossible for the Church of Rome to change its doctrine on this issue.

Once I realized the eternal consistency of Catholic doctrine on the sanctity of life, it just didn't make sense to remain outside the Church anymore.

There were still teachings of the Catholic Church that I didn't understand, like purgatory. And then there was devotion to the Virgin Mary. However much I wanted to be like St. Maximilian in everything, something within me resisted thinking of Mary the way he did, as "Mom." On the

Chesterton tour, the "have you heard of Edith Stein" crowd tried to help me appreciate Church teachings on Mary by suggesting I think of her as my "Jewish mother." Besides annoying the heck out of me—if I were black, would they tell me Mary was my Mammy?—that only aggravated the problem, since the popular stereotype of Jewish mothers is that they are controlling. What's more, I had a Jewish mother of my own—one who, unlike Mary, no longer wanted to be involved with the Catholic Church.

But I had an overwhelming feeling that the Catholic Church was the only home left for me. Even if, upon arriving there, I still wasn't happy, there was no other place where I could be. The saints were there. Any truth to be found was grounded there. So Jesus must be there in a manner in which he wasn't present anywhere else. And if he was there, I would not be satisfied unless I was there, too.

So on February 16 I went to Mass at Our Saviour Catholic Church, near Grand Central Terminal. Fr. Rutler's homily was about Fátima, which interested me because it was an appearance of the Virgin Mary that took place in modern times. I was astonished to learn that the last living Fátima visionary, Sr. Lucia, had only just died at ninety-seven—about the age my Grandma Mimi would be if she were still alive.

Afterward, I approached Fr. Rutler when he was greeting parishioners at the door and blurted out, "I've just been fired from the *New York Post* and I want to enter the Catholic Church." He laughed and said those two things didn't normally go together. Then he recommended I contact the parish secretary to enroll in RCIA.

I did as Father instructed. February went by, March too—no response. Although I was eager to be in the Church, it seemed the Church wasn't so eager to have me.

Finally, one evening in April, I was having dinner at a midtown restaurant with John Zmirak, a Catholic writer I know from the conservative scene, and told him of my failed attempt to come home to Rome. He replied that, given my hunger for orthodoxy and my being more knowledgeable about the faith than most non-Catholics, I would be unhappy in most RCIA programs.

RCIA, John explained, really stood for Repelling Catholics InAdvertently. To avoid having a bad experience, I should approach Fr. Jacek Buda, a Polish Dominican friar at the Church of Notre Dame, near Columbia University; he was highly literate and liked journalists.

It took another couple of months before I could garner the courage to risk another rejection. But finally I did, and I'm glad, because now Fr. Buda is on the line and ready to make time in his schedule to see me this very week.

I reach down to pick up my purse and take out my datebook so Fr. and I can set up an appointment. As I do, my gaze falls upon the small icon of St. Maximilian Kolbe that adorns my desk. I'd really like to have a cross there too but am worried about offending co-workers.

It's all set now; Fr. Buda has agreed to meet me Wednesday morning before I go to work. After I hang up the phone, I find myself unconsciously reaching for the pewter cross that hangs from a chain around my neck. *Thank you, God.*

What was I doing when Father called? Oh, yes, finishing up the first round of page proofs; they're right here.

Five minutes later. Page proofs are done.

My supervisor Bob doesn't have any work for me right now, so I walk over to the table where competing newspapers are set out daily and pick up a copy of the *Times* to take back to my cubicle. But when I put the first section on my desk and unfold it, there is little I can do but stare at it and hope my co-workers think I'm reading. Until Bob gives me more work, I have too much on my mind to do anything but ruminate.

It felt so subversive to receive a call at the *News* from a Catholic priest.

Upon my hiring two months ago, I thought I would be safe from persecution, especially having the support of the two top editors. There was an awkward moment, shortly after I started on the job, when Bob revealed to me he was openly gay. I thought he might be angry over my blog entries opposing the gay agenda. But he quickly assuaged my fears; he grew up among people with traditional views on sexuality, he said, and he didn't begrudge me mine. He was in fact so kind and so tolerant of my beliefs that I felt convicted, as the words "kind" and "tolerant" don't always apply to my *Dawn Patrol* writings.

But my perceptions of safety changed a few weeks ago when Bob revealed to me that several gay employees—he himself not among them—had together submitted a letter to the editor-in-chief to complain about a recent *Dawn Patrol* post.

I had been blogging while angry. That was my first mistake.

The post concerned a condom maker's plan to distribute 100,000 condoms to local shops for free, ostensibly to help fight AIDS. I wrote that the plan was emblematic of a larger problem in which those seeking to prevent homosexuals' deaths were instead giving them a false sense of safety. Instead of promoting condoms, which have a high failure rate, they should be promoting abstinence.

So my intentions were good. I was concerned because "gay men I cared about, including a close personal friend, died from AIDS because their community fostered an 'and the band played on' lifestyle, encouraging so-called 'safe' or 'safer' sex."

But in my anger as well as my desire to win attention, I went too heavy on the sarcasm. Responding to the condom maker's boast that it was "protecting" New York City, I wrote, "Oh, yeah, my city's really protected now. All those sodomites can rest easy knowing that their chances of infecting one another with HIV are reduced to only 13 to 20 percent."

That was my second mistake.

After meetings with Bob—who was once more perfectly tolerant and forgiving—and with the editors, the situation was resolved. I removed all references to "sodomy" and "sodomites" on my blog and promised to moderate my language in future.

However, at least one person on staff wasn't satisfied with the resolution. One of our art department's artists quietly informed me that even if my bosses were willing to let bygones be bygones after I whitewashed my blog, he and certain colleagues of his wouldn't let me off so easily. Someone had printed out copies of my original Dawn Patrol entries and put them in a file to keep them at hand if my name ever came up for promotion.

So—*sigh*—although I'm better off than when the *Post* fired me, once again it's looking like I may not have the bright future in New York City media that I was hoping for.

Friday, April 14, 2006, 7:57 p.m. Oh, good, they haven't started yet. Made it just in time. I lost a few minutes when I stopped to buy an umbrella from a street vendor, but now I am here outside St. Patrick's Old Cathedral on Mott Street for the annual Way of the Cross procession through downtown Manhattan.

It looks like about eighty other young adults are here too,

along with a priest in a very cool-looking old-fashioned cape, a Franciscan friar, and Vince, a seminarian I recognize from Our Saviour.

I am still thinking about yesterday afternoon and evening. I can't not think about it. It was so beautiful. Fr. Buda received me into the Church at noon and then, six hours later, at Holy Thursday Mass, I received my First Communion.

The reception ceremony was private—just me, Fr. Buda, and one other already-baptized catechumen. It will be different at my Confirmation on Holy Saturday, when Mom and Ron will be there along with my friend Julia, who is sponsoring me. But I didn't mind at all not having others there; it made the ceremony feel more intimate between myself and God. Father gave a brief homily in which he quoted a passage from Fr. Richard John Neuhaus that touched me:

> To those of you with whom I have traveled in the past, know that we travel together still. In the mystery of Christ and his Church nothing is lost, and the broken will be mended. If, as I am persuaded, my communion with Christ's Church is now the fuller, then it follows that my unity with all who are in Christ is now the stronger. We travel together still.

Although I realize Neuhaus was referring to those who shared his former faith of Lutheranism, his words express what I hope for my relationships with all my friends and family who are not Catholic or are not practicing Catholics. I hope and pray that, now that I am in full communion with the Church, I may be closer to them.

My knowledge of Catholic theology is still only beginning, so I could be wrong, but somehow I feel as though anyone who grows in union with Christ has to grow in union with other human beings too. It just makes sense, because Christ became man to bring us closer not only to God but also to one another. And I do believe that my reception into the Church added something to my union with Christ. I was united with him before, through my baptism, but there is something different now, something new, something I needed.

Vince passes me a photocopied sheet with prayers and song lyrics, and a young woman hands me a candle. Just before we begin the first station right outside St. Patrick's, the rain stops. A good sign.

Thirteen minutes later. The street sign next to our second station says Margaret Sanger Square. We are praying next to Planned Parenthood's New York City headquarters.

One of the young men says, "We adore you, O Christ, and we praise you."

Then we all get down on one knee—I mean, genuflect—and say, "Because by your Holy Cross you have redeemed the world."

Yes, Lord. You have redeemed the world. And you have redeemed me, bringing me into communion with these people who seek to answer hatred with love.

About three hours later. Thus far we have walked through the Lower East Side and the East Village, and are now well into the West Village—as far east as Tompkins Square Park and as far north as Union Square Park. Wherever we go, the wooden cross goes first, lifted high by one of the men. A few other participants carry tall torches, which also serve to relight our candles. Many of us are carrying palm leaves; a few palm leaves are also draped around the cross.

Most of our stations have been outside Catholic churches,

including a Spanish-language one, a Polish one, and one that I think was Slovenian. I am awed by the diversity of ethnic churches within a few square miles; truly I have entered a universal faith.

As we walk, we sing. I miss the Protestant hymns. Other than "Were You There," our songs aren't really songs so much as chants: "*Ave Maria,*" "*Misericordias Domini,*" "*Ubi Caritas,*" "*Salve Regina,*" and "Our Father." According to the printout, they are "Taize"; I must look up what that means. Wish someone would sing "Amazing Grace."

On the upside, no one has yet volunteered "Awesome God."

We have walked past Weinstein dormitory, my old NYU home. We went through the streets where I had been so unhappy as a college student, suffering from depression and believing that if there were a God, he didn't care about me. We proceeded within a hundred feet of where a young woman whose name I will never know handed me the pocket Gideons New Testament/Psalms/Proverbs that I held onto throughout the years when I questioned whether God cared about me, if he even existed.

We walk on past posters for Madonna's latest tour, which is called "Confessions." We sing praises to God in Latin as we pass shops with names like The Shape of Lies. We chant about Jesus as we walk past the werewolf-themed Slaughtered Lamb Pub. We sing "Ave Maria" all the way down Christopher Street, past the hangouts for men cruising for gay sex and past the display windows filled with black leather and chains.

Feelings of sadness come to me. I wish I had known of the beauty of the Church in college and saved myself years of wandering in the wilderness. But then it occurs to me that God must have known what he was doing. Perhaps if

I had entered the Church back then, I wouldn't have had a strong enough foundation to cleave to it. Also, my relationships with some of my family members have deepened since that time; loved ones accept my conversion who might have distanced themselves from me had I converted back then.

As the procession winds its way through the Village, our songs echoing through the darkened streets, I have the feeling that we are bringing salt and light—and an unmistakable sword.

A mental image comes to me, the same one I had last night when I had my First Communion. It's an image of the globe of the Earth. I see it as being sheathed in darkness, but every so often a patch of light breaks through. The picture brings to mind patches of new, healed skin emerging on a leper—and the healing keeps leading to more healing.

It feels so radical to take back the streets with song and prayer. We aren't blocking anyone, we aren't accosting anyone. All we are doing is being a living witness to Jesus' love and lordship.

I am so thankful to be part of a Church that witnesses so boldly, peacefully, and powerfully. I want to pray outside abortion clinics now. I want to make processions everywhere.

One young drunk asked us what we were doing; when someone told him, he said, "It *is* a good Friday!" Another young man, as we passed by, made a big show of saying, "I'm not with these guys, I have nothing to do with these guys." A young, fashionable-looking woman eating inside a restaurant put her fork down and turned her head to the window, mystified by the parade. Another woman who looked to be in her forties—which is old for the Village—stopped as we passed her, smiling with apparent approval.

After singing and chanting our way down Christopher

Street, we did the twelfth station outside St. Veronica's Church on Christopher Street, across from the Archives building, where Monica Lewinsky lives. Now we are approaching St. Vincent's Hospital to observe the thirteenth station at the Wall of Hope and Remembrance.

During the hours and days shortly after 9/11, throughout New York City people posted flyers with photographs, names, and personal details about their loved ones who were missing in the wake of the terrorist attacks. Here at St. Vincent's, one of the hospitals closest to the World Trade Center site, an entire outside wall was covered with such flyers, each bearing a précis of a life. After the last survivor was treated and it became clear that nearly all those who had been listed as missing had died, the hospital decided to let the flyers remain on the wall, preserved under protective glass, as a memorial.

"We adore you, O Christ, and we praise you."

"Because by your Holy Cross you have redeemed the world."

"The thirteenth station. Jesus is taken down from the cross."

As I listen to Vince read St. Alphonsus Liguori's account of the moment when Jesus' body was placed in Mary's arms, my eyes fall upon the peeling flyers wallpapered beneath the glass. Many of the images of the victims are from family photos. The happiness on their faces adds an extra level of poignancy. I strain to make out the names that go with the smiling faces: Cesar R. Garcia, Evelyn McKinnedy, George Merkouris. A verse comes to mind; I don't know where it comes from: "united with him in a death like his."

Some of the responsorial lines at each station sound like a variation of the Sinner's Prayer: "I am sorry that I have offended you. Never let me offend you again. Grant that I may love you always; and then do with me as you will."

Yes, Lord, I am sorry. Help me, Lord.

Twelve minutes later. It is close to midnight. We are praying the final station outside St. Joseph's on Sixth Avenue and Washington Place. I have been inside the building as a volunteer; the church donates its basement to the Caring Community, which prepares meals that are delivered to the elderly and shut-ins. But I have never before come here to pray.

One last genuflection for the night. One last prayer from St. Alphonsus, this one asking to share in Jesus' resurrection. One last request to love Jesus always. One last verse from the *Stabat Mater.*

The last note from our singing fades into the urban air. There is a moment of silence. Then a young man who had sung in a fine tenor voice says out loud the words from John's Gospel that I have been thinking:

"And the light shines in the darkness, and the darkness did not comprehend it."

Wednesday, December 26, 2007, 3:55 p.m. I feel guilty for telling my former *Daily News* colleague Sarah that I had to rush to catch my train. If I had only taken a moment to dash out of the dining court and check the big board, I would have known that my train back to Washington, D.C., is running at least ten minutes late.

It was so good of Sarah to take time out of her workday to have coffee with me here at Penn Station. In fact, this whole visit to New York has been wonderful. I miss my old friends. It meant a lot to catch up with them and to attend the beautiful Midnight Mass at the Church of Notre Dame.

Too bad I now have to get back to the rest of my life.

Just five days left of 2007. This really has not been the best of years. If it weren't for its being my first full year as a Catholic, I would be tempted to trade it in.

The year began with me facing multiple stresses at work and at home. At the *News*, with Bob having been promoted, I was now working for a different boss, leading my comfort level to plunge.

Of all people, the editors had me work under a man who previously had been in formation as a Jesuit in India. He was filled with anger against the Church. I remember especially what he said when I mentioned that some group that wanted us to give them press was a cult. He responded, "If we're going to accuse groups of being cults, we should apply the same standard to other religions, like those whose people abuse little boys."

It seemed too that the publication of my first book, *The Thrill of the Chaste*, led the *News* to become a less friendly place for me. Although the book made a big splash in the media, even making the Sunday Styles section of the *New York Times*, my own paper made no mention of it whatsoever. It was as though the *News* was embarrassed to have one of its editors publicly proclaim that, in the words of the *Sunday Times* of London's headline to an article I wrote, "casual sex is a con."

At home, I was suffering interiorly from my self-imposed separation from Mom and Ron, which began during the summer of last year. It came about after my stress at work led me to seek counseling. Although the "Catholic psychologist" I saw wasn't the best—I later discovered his doctorate was from an unaccredited institution—he asked the right questions.

With "Dr." Mango's guidance, I came to see that my anxiety was connected to the abuse I had suffered in childhood. Until then, although I knew that painful things were done to me in the past, I hadn't begun to consider how they had affected me, or even the extent to which they were wrong.

Now I saw that the abuse had not only wounded me personally but also damaged my relationships with my parents.

The greatest damage was to my relationship with Mom. I resented her for having failed to protect me from her depraved boyfriend Henry.

Mango recommended I talk with Mom about the lingering hurt I felt from the abuse. But when I tried, not only did it not help, it actually made things worse. When I brought up what happened, she couldn't remember all the abuses I remembered. Then, when I insisted my memories were valid, she started crying; it was more than she could bear.

I felt at once guilty for having unsettled Mom and frustrated at being unable to gain closure. Neither could I look to Ron to help her understand me, as he had sometimes done in the past on the rare occasions when Mom and I disagreed about something. On this issue, they were a united front: I had revived past pain to no good purpose.

Why did I even feel the need to have Mom grieve with me over what I had suffered? Mango posed that question to me and offered a blunt answer: I was emotionally "enmeshed" with my mother, even "in thrall" to her.

My therapist's words were difficult to take, but upon reflection I came to believe he was essentially right. My relationship with my mother had always been intense, even overwhelming. Many women say their mother is their best friend, but mine literally was. I was emotionally dependent upon her in such a way that the normal boundaries between mother and child were blurred. The more I thought about it, the more I realized that I barely even knew where I stopped and she began.

It was different when I was living in Hoboken and just seeing Mom on weekends. Although we talked nearly every day, and I felt guilty if I didn't fill her in on every detail of

my emotional life, at least I had a sense that I was in com-
mand of my world.

But then came the time last year, shortly before I started seeing Dr. Mango, when I was looking to buy my own
home for the first time, and Mom and Ron convinced me
to choose a place just across town from them. Not that I
needed much convincing. A Morristown condo would be
far less expensive than a Hoboken one, and I'd have an easy
rail commute to my friends and job in New York.

Unfortunately the condo came with Seventies-style wall-
to-wall carpeting that smelled like cigarette smoke. I opted
to have the rugs torn out in favor of Hoboken-style hard-
wood floors. Mom thoughtfully volunteered to let in the
contractors, saving me from having to miss work.

On the day the contractors were to have finished, as I
walked the last few steps home from the train station after
a long day at the *News*, the thought of entering my newly
beautified condo filled me with joy.

True, even if the new floors came out perfectly, the unit
wouldn't yet look like a dream home. As usual, I hadn't
bothered to make my bed. Most of my things were still in
boxes. But even so, it was exciting to be coming home for
the first time in my life to a place that was truly my own.

The living room looked just as I had hoped. But when I
walked into my bedroom, I found that the bed I had left in
disarray was now neatly made, with a new bedspread and a
large teddy bear propped up on the pillow. Mom had taken it
upon herself to top off the contractors' work with a surprise.

For a split second, I stood there dumbly, staring at my bed
and processing what had happened. Here I had imagined I
was genuinely independent for the first time in my life. Seeing that teddy bear made me feel instead as though I'd been
thrust back into a crib, or even the womb.

I felt angry at Mom for reasons I didn't fully understand and still don't. And I was angry at myself for being angry at her. And for the first time for a long time, I had to restrain the urge to hurt myself.

At that moment, I knew that if I was ever to have an identity apart from my mother, I had to step back. But given the dynamics of our relationship, I didn't know of any way I could do that without making a hard break.

The wound in my relationship with my father was less complex but still painful. I believed I wouldn't have been abused if he had been more present during my childhood and had properly monitored my home life with Mom.

Mango's best idea was to have my father join me for a therapy session. It impressed me that Dad was willing to make the trip from D.C., to sit with me, to listen and learn about the impact that his personal disengagement had upon my young life. For his part, he was deeply affected when I described to him the abuses I suffered, all of which—even the incidents with Al at the temple—were news to him. By the end of the session, I felt closer to him than I had during my whole adult life.

By the spring of this year, there wasn't much to tie me to my job or home. That's when a friend who knew I needed guidance put me in touch with Fr. C. John McCloskey, a priest of Opus Dei based in Washington, D.C., who was famous for guiding Catholic converts.

Fr. McCloskey told me there was no need for me to endure persecution at the *Daily News* when I could move to Washington, be near Dad and Linda, and have my pick of workplaces where Catholics were welcome. What's more, he said, D.C. was an ideal place for a young Catholic adult, with many opportunities for spiritual growth and fellowship.

It seemed at first that Fr. McCloskey's advice was truly the will of God. Soon after I began exploring the D.C. job market, I was hired by the Cardinal Newman Society, a Virginia nonprofit that wanted me to develop programs to promote chastity on Catholic college campuses. I quit the *News*, moved to Washington, became productive in my Newman position, sold my Morristown condo, and was set to close on a co-op apartment one block from my father's and stepmother's home.

Everything was perfect. And then it fell apart.

Five months after I began at Newman, the society's president decided to scrap the chastity program. He offered to keep me on in a different position, but the new assignment was well outside my range of interests. So, fifteen days ago, I found myself without a job—just as I was about to close on my purchase of the apartment.

I opted to close anyway. The apartment was too good to lose, plus I had already made a nonrefundable payment to hold it for purchase. If God is in this somewhere, then he will take care of me. I hope—I mean, I believe he will.

And I'm not even going to think about the biopsy I had last week of the lump on my thyroid, because I have enough to think about already. And anyway, it was a bit much for the doctor to insist on a biopsy when my previous endocrinologist biopsied it several years ago and it proved benign.

Sigh. Now the big board is saying my train is twenty minutes late. Might as well pull out my cellphone and call into my home voicemail to see if anyone is trying to reach me there. Maybe an employer has called back, though it's not likely, given that this is Christmas week.

My outgoing message kicks in on the second ring. That means I have a voicemail. I punch the star key and my password.

"Hello, Dawn, this is Dr. Sadeghi. I need to discuss your biopsy results with you, and I'm going to have to see you. Please call me today."

12 Along Comes Mary

Friday, February 1, 2008, 5:36 p.m. Which scarf to wear? I would need one tonight even if my neck weren't stitched up.

I'll wear the black pashmina-style one. It's soft and it goes with everything.

Should I bring a Percocet just in case I need it? No. Better not. Must try to keep my dosage down to one at a time. I needed two at a time when I was in the hospital, but since coming home I have managed to go down to just one, thank God. I don't want to become addicted.

Not needing too much pain medication—that's another answer to prayer. I've had so many answered prayers this past week. Need to keep track so I can remember to be grateful when I am feeling stressed about my health and about dealing with all the inconveniences that go with being a patient.

Should I eat a banana before I leave? I had so many emails to answer this afternoon, thanking friends and Dawn Patrol readers who were praying for my recovery, that I forgot to eat, and now I'm starving.

Might as well. My stepmother Linda said we would order from Meiwah once I arrive. So it is probably at least half an hour before I'll actually be sitting down to eat with her and Dad.

I'm still thinking about how beautiful it was to see my family's concern for me when I entered the hospital Tuesday morning. Dad and Linda were there along with Jennifer, who traveled from Cincinnati to be with me. They tried to buoy my spirits, but, like me, they were all concerned because the results of the biopsy of my thyroid lump were "suspicious." When the intake receptionist put the band on my wrist, I thought about how Dad could remember the day in 1968 when Uncle Irving—Mom's obstetrician—put a band on me.

Mom and Ron were at the hospital in spirit. They would have come down from New Jersey if I had let them, but I was afraid it would be too much for me.

I'm still not ready to see them apart from family gatherings—especially now that, with the help of my psychiatrist, I have a better understanding of why certain things they do set me off. Thank God I finally received an accurate diagnosis after so many years of my being misdiagnosed. And that wouldn't have happened if I hadn't moved to D.C. More divine providence!

My psychiatrist informed me that I have complex posttraumatic stress disorder. With his help, I am beginning to learn how to cope with it, becoming conscious of the things that trigger me.

What is helping me most is learning to distinguish between objective reality and the distorted perceptions caused by my emotional flashbacks. If I can accomplish that, then there is hope for greater stability in every area of my life—jobs, relationships—because I won't feel the temptation to act impulsively or defensively as I have in the past.

While I'm counting my blessings, I should also thank God for the consolation I received through the anointing of the sick.

My pastor, Msgr. Filardi, was the one who suggested I receive the sacrament in advance of my surgery. It hadn't occurred to me to ask for it; I thought it was only for people with life-threatening illnesses. But Monsignor said that, since general anesthesia carried a risk of death, there was legitimate reason for him to anoint me.

Never before was I so happy at a sentence containing the words "risk of death." *You did this to me, God, making me a Catholic. If I weren't, none of this would make sense.*

What especially excited me about the anointing was that I had recently read Archbishop Fulton J. Sheen's booklet *Calvary and the Mass* and was deeply moved by it. Sheen says we should never have any "wasted pain." Rather, we should offer all our sufferings to Jesus in union with his own sufferings, so that his merits may become ours and our merits may participate in his redemption of humanity.

When Monsignor anointed me—especially when he touched the sacred oil to the palms of my hands, reminding me of the wounds Jesus suffered in his Passion—Sheen's words came back to me. I felt assured that, when I went under the knife, none of my sufferings would be wasted. God would receive them on behalf of those for whom I was offering them.

Then there was the blessing of having my surgery at the hospital that is part of the medical school where my father was a professor and administrator for nearly thirty years. My doctors there all knew and respected Dad. One of the third-year medical residents who was to take part in my surgery told me that my father was like a mentor to him.

My big prayer as I was wheeled into the operating room was for the conversion of all my family, including that my mother would return to the Church and take my stepfather Ron with her.

I would not want to relive the moment I woke up from the operation. My neck stung and the stitches felt as though they were too tight. But that was the worst of it. All went well; I spent the night in a private room and by the next afternoon was home and answering email.

The most moving email by far was the one from Mom. She wrote of something that happened to her at Ron's optometry practice, where she works as a therapist:

A woman came into our office at the time you were in surgery. I had met her only once, several months ago. She asked me to hold out my hand. She had her hand tightly closed, opening it into my hand. There was an olive-wood rosary in it.

She had had this rosary on her night table and had been praying with it every night. She said, "I didn't want to go out today, but I thought that I had to bring this to you, that you needed it." . . . She also shared her devotion to the Lord.

I told her that you were undergoing surgery just at that moment, and that I was just at that moment looking for someone with whom I could share my anxious and helpless feeling about it.

I told her that you pray the rosary, and she said, "Now you have to pray it for her, because she can't."

Although I felt strange doing so, I remembered how to do it, and I prayed for you.

Thank God, He answered my prayers.

Love,

Mommy

Reading Mom's email, I felt my prayers had been answered too.

I responded with a thank-you, writing as warmly as I could. Best to wait until another day to renew my complaint over her still wanting me, at age thirty-nine, to call her "Mommy."

It's amazing how God works things out. I had thought he brought me to Washington because he wanted me to work for the Cardinal Newman Society. But now it looks like he willed that I come here for my health. Had I remained in New York City and sought surgery there, it's unlikely I would have received such a high level of care.

What else am I thankful for? Of course, my new job. It's not really a *job* job, just freelance work writing and editing at a think tank. But it will pay my bills for the next several months, and hopefully a permanent position will arise by then.

Must leave my apartment now. I told Linda I would be over at 5:45.

Locking my door. I might as well take the stairs down and not wait for the elevator; it's just one flight.

No one else is in earshot as I exit my building onto Twenty-fourth Street Northwest, so I can speak out loud and discover how my voice sounds this evening: "Thank you, God. Thank you, God."

It sounds raw. But it's better than it was this morning and better than it was yesterday. *I do thank you, God, that I still have a voice.* My big fear going into the operation was the small but significant risk that my laryngeal nerve might be damaged.

I still have part of my thyroid. The initial pathology results, done while I remained under anesthesia, were inconclusive, so the surgeon gave Dad the opportunity to make the call over whether I should have a full thyroidectomy.

Dad asked the surgeon what he would do if he were making the decision over his own thyroid, and he replied that he would opt for retaining what was left of it. The doctor noted that I was in good health and so could stand for a second operation if need be. Moreover, if the pathology revealed that the second operation wasn't needed, I would avoid having to get radioactive-iodine treatment, which would have been necessary had my full thyroid been removed.

So now I am waiting for the final pathology report. Dad knows the pathologist, and I've authorized my medical team to share my information with him, so he will have the results before I do.

It's times like this that I wish I could call Sr. Gerry, the blind Filippini Sister I met at the religious order's New Jersey retreat house back when I was writing *The Thrill of the Chaste*. She's been gone now for . . . what, a year? And the pain is still fresh.

Darn. Just the thought of that holy old nun made me tear up. Must dry my eyes once I get inside Dad and Linda's apartment building and can take off my gloves. I don't want them to see me crying.

If anyone knew how to have cancer, it was Sr. Gerry. She had lived with blindness since her twenties, accomplishing beautiful things as a teacher, author, poet, and songwriter, when the illness struck. At the time I encountered her, her body was suffering the effects of several aggressive tumors. Yet her presence radiated an impossible joy. It was the glow of a woman who has asked the Lord with all her heart to make her an instrument of his peace. Her eyes sparkled in a way that I've never witnessed in a blind person before or since.

Approaching the building now. Up the elevator. I hope Dad and Linda's new puppy Yoffi isn't in a jumpy mood.

Dear God, whatever you have in store for me, please let me receive it as Sr. Gerry would.

Dad greets me with a hug, careful not to put pressure on my neck. Linda hugs me too and hands me the Chinese-takeout menu.

I take a seat on one of the stools in their cozy eat-in kitchen with the lovely granite countertop. Pink granite always reminds me of the large rocks where Dad and I used to sit behind our house in Galveston, overlooking the bay, when I was a small child. When Dad cast his fishing line into the waters, he would encourage me to sing to the fish. He said it made them bite. So I would sing all the songs I knew. Then Dad would tell me my song was working as he reeled in a catch, and I would feel a surge of pride.

Dad asks if I would like a glass of wine. The question warms my heart, and not because I'm all that fond of alcohol. Somehow, even though I am nearing forty, I never feel so grown-up as I do when one of my parents invites me to have a drink with dinner.

It is a little odd, though, that Dad would offer me a drink before dinner. Also, he knows I'm on Percocet. But then again, he knows I don't drink to excess, so one glass of wine is not going to harm me. And even if it does, the hospital is just down the street.

Nice that they have white Zinfandel. Linda remembered that it's one of the only wines I drink. She adds ice to make it go easy on my throat.

Dad clears his throat. He has a gift for being calm under pressure, but even so, he is not very good at hiding things. I have an idea of what is coming.

He tells me I have multifocal papillary thyroid carcinoma and also Hashimoto's disease.

The good news, he says, is that "the margins are good," so the cancer—cancer!—has not metastasized, thank God. And the Hashimoto's will disappear when my thyroid does. So my doctor expects that, once I have the rest of my thyroid removed and receive radioactive-iodine therapy, I will be completely cured.

Dad has a way of making everything sound so positive that I almost don't mind the parts about having the rest of my thyroid removed and receiving radioactive-iodine therapy.

I do have so much to be thankful for, especially family and friends who love me. Which is a good thing, because no sooner will the scar on my throat begin to heal than I will have to go through the whole operation again and, a few months afterward, get nuked.

Wednesday, February 13, 2008, 7:51 p.m. I shouldn't be nervous. The talk I'm about to give will be at least my fiftieth lecture on chastity since *The Thrill of the Chaste* came out.

But as members of Georgetown University's chapters of the Catholic Daughters of America, InterVarsity, and Knights of Columbus, along with theology professor Fr. Stephen Fields, S.J., lead me to Room 107 in the Intercultural Center, my heart beats anxiously.

The nation's oldest Jesuit college is known for many things, but these days chastity is not one of them. I am still pondering what I learned twenty minutes ago over dinner at The Tombs, when the sponsors of my talk told me that a posse of student volunteers known as "condom fairies" left envelopes containing free prophylactics outside the doors of dorm rooms.

"And the RAs"—resident advisers—"permit that?" I asked.

"Some of the condom fairies *are* the RAs," a student replied.

What I am really afraid of are anti-chastity demonstrators. When I worked for the Cardinal Newman Society, my boss told me that when he spoke at Georgetown, he was met by angry women wearing t-shirts advertising the feminist play "Vagina Monologues."

Maybe I will be lucky and the condom fairies will forgo my talk in favor of the competing one across campus by Republican Congressman Ron Paul. Anyway, I'm told that Room 107 only holds sixty people, so the crowd's size won't be too daunting.

Here we are at the classroom. I peer inside. All the seats are full. Students are sitting on the floor. And Dad made good on his promise to come; he's at a desk in the back.

I don't see any protest signs or offensive t-shirts. What I do see is the most diverse audience I have ever encountered. It's a true cross-section of Georgetown's population.

And, I realize, they want to hear me tell them something that will help them navigate the world of relationships, including their relationship with God.

But I'm no use to them in my current state. Must put on spiritual armor—and quickly.

I turn to Fr. Fields. It would have been good if I had thought of this before dinner.

"Father, would it be possible for me to make a quick confession?"

"I think we can do that," he responds. "Let's go down the hall."

He leads me down some corridors until we find a place that is not directly in the path students are taking to reach Room 107.

"Bless me, Father, for I have sinned. It has been"—how long since my anointing?—"just over two weeks since my last confession."

I reel off my transgressions. Mostly they're the same boring ones I always confess, but there is one particular sin that has been nagging at me.

It feels good to get it all out before I open up to students about my past life. I want the state of grace that Jesus will give me through Father's absolution.

The more I give talks, the more I learn how important it is to speak in a spirit of love. There is always a point in my talks where I have to identify sin for what it is, and I have a hard time doing that without sounding resentful—or, worse, jealous—of people who are what I once was. But God is helping me.

Almost done. But there's one more thing. There always is.

"And I want to tell God I'm sorry for all the times I haven't been grateful this past couple of weeks."

I need to keep remembering all the good things God is doing, especially how he is blessing me with the prayers of so many people, even from readers I may never meet. Just a few days ago, when Dad called and asked me how I was doing, I told him it was the happiest time of my life. And I meant it.

When I have finished, Fr. Fields says, "You've made a good confession. And for your penance . . ."

He thinks for a moment.

"Down the hall," Father resumes, "there is a room full of students. I would like you to go into that room and give the students a talk on chastity. Can you do that?"

Tuesday, July 7, 2008, 1:17 p.m. Seated at the desk before me in this closet-sized office is a bespectacled

Dominican priest with hair as white as his habit, his figure backlit by the sunlight streaming through the window behind him.

"Thank you so much for making time to see me," I begin.

It's been a long time since I've felt this nervous in a school administrator's office. Plus this isn't just any school; it's the Dominican House of Studies, and its primary mission is to prepare Dominican seminarians for the priesthood.

"I really appreciate your willingness to consider my application so close to the start of the school year."

Fr. Gabriel O'Donnell glances up from the sheet of paper he is holding in his right hand; it contains my GRE scores. I am glad to see a copy of *The Thrill of the Chaste* on his desk; it must be the one I mailed him.

"Well," he says, "being that we're a seminary and a pontifical faculty, we often have bishops asking us if we can accept students this time of year, particularly if they're priests who have just finished their studies in Rome. The academic year there doesn't end until the end of June."

"I see."

Fr. O'Donnell picks up another paper from his desk and visually scans it. As far as I can make out, it is my application.

"So," he says, and his word hangs in the air for a moment. "Your background is in journalism. Why are you seeking to do a master's degree in theology?"

I want so much to give him a formal, polished answer, the kind that would go over well in a corporate job interview. But try as I may, my reply sounds scattershot. There's just too much information to relate, and much of it is intense: becoming Christian . . . becoming Catholic . . . wanting to work in a place where I won't be under attack for my faith

. . . becoming an author and speaker . . . thyroid cancer . . .
joblessness . . . needing health insurance.

Hope that last point didn't sound mercenary. But how else
can I put it? It's true. My experience of cancer has shown me
that full-time freelancing is not a viable option. I need to get
a job that provides health insurance, and having a graduate
degree will increase my chances.

Fr. O'Donnell's eyes are starting to glaze over; time to
wrap up my monologue. Waving my hands animatedly, I
try to sound modest as I boast of the popularity of *The Thrill
of the Chaste* and how it has made me an in-demand speaker on college campuses. That in turn leads me to believe I
might have a future in campus ministry, for which I would
need a theology M.A.

All that is left now is to explain why I chose Dominican
House. I tell how impressed I am with the knowledge of the
Dominican friars I've met who have studied there. Also, I
admire Archbishop Fulton J. Sheen, so I would like to study
what he studied: the theology of St. Thomas Aquinas.

That last line about Sheen is adequate for a grand finale. I
smile and let my hands rest.

Fr. O'Donnell adjusts his glasses and looks again at one of
the papers before him. "Looking at your GRE results, you
scored well in the verbal and quantitative sections. Then
there is your score on the writing section, which is surpris-
ing; it's below average . . . "

"Oh!" I exclaim. "I was surprised by that too! Maybe the
grader didn't like that I wrote on my conversion."

Well, that was a dumb thing to say—alleging anti-Cath-
olic bias rather than owning up to my own failings. Perhaps
Fr. O'Donnell will be generous and chalk it up to nerves,
but I'd better correct myself quickly. "More likely I was
overconfident."

"Well, looking at it, I just thought, with your being an author, you must know how to write. So we'll assume it was just some kind of fluke."

Monday, August 25, 2008, 11:10 a.m. I need air. I need water. I need something cold. Feeling faint, hot, dizzy.

It's okay. Calm down. This is normal. The doctors told me I might have these symptoms. Anyway, now that the registrar has finished giving us new students a tour of Dominican House, I have twenty minutes before the Mass of the Holy Spirit that opens the school year. So there's time to relax and to try to feel better.

My body has been through so much in just a few months. There was my second thyroid operation back in May. No sooner was I back up to speed than I had to go off my thyroid medication for weeks in preparation for my radioactive-iodine therapy, which was necessary so that any remaining thyroid cells in my body might be destroyed. For weeks I felt sluggish and uncomfortable.

Now, just four days after completing the radioactive-iodine therapy, I'm back on the thyroid hormone—but taking a higher dose than before, in order to get my metabolism back up to speed. That, and my excitement about my first day at Dominican House, made it hard to sleep last night. So I shouldn't worry about my symptoms; they're normal for someone whose body has been made to suffer a hormonal see-saw.

Thank God the freezer in the cramped student lounge has ice. I find a white Styrofoam cup and fill it with cubes, then add water from the metal sink.

Better grab a napkin too. I might need it, as I just used up my last tissue.

Down the stairs. This building that houses both the Dominican priory and Dominican House of Studies—I have to get used to calling it what the dean said this morning is its full official name, the *Pontifical Faculty of the Immaculate Conception* at the Dominican House of Studies—is a century old and it shows. I'm feeling sensitive to the dust and the general musty old-building smell.

Please, God, don't let me come down with a migraine. I've only had migraines twice. That's enough for a lifetime.

Outside at last. I can sit on the front steps, where it's shady, and gaze at the Basilica of the National Shrine of the Immaculate Conception across Michigan Avenue.

Big sip of water. That feels better. I must need the water, because I'm sweating.

Sweating! How strange it is to imagine that I have radioactive sweat. That's what the note in my purse from my doctor says.

When the hospital released me last Thursday after my two days in isolation for the radioactive-iodine therapy, the doctor made a point of telling me he was giving me a signed note as evidence that I had just received radiation.

I responded that there was no need for him to go to the trouble; being unemployed, I wouldn't have to provide anyone with proof of why I missed work. But he explained that the letter would be necessary for me in case I passed through any radiation detectors; they have such detectors in the Metro system, he said. It was possible, he said, that I might set one off and need to prove to the police that I wasn't a terrorist. That was a scary thought.

Thankfully no alarm sirens went off as I passed through the Metro turnstiles on my way here this morning. I spent my ride surreptitiously drinking a bottle of Diet Pepsi and eating a granola bar—unlike in New York, they actually arrest people here for eating on the train—and rereading the doctor's note. It said I was given I-131 at 2:45 p.m. August 19 with a half-life extending over 8.1 days. That means I will remain radioactive until 2.4 hours after 2:45 p.m. this Wednesday, August 27. On that day, I can look forward to entering a full-body MRI machine for a post-operative scan . . . *sigh*.

The good news is that, as of yesterday, my radiation level is low enough that I can sit next to people for a few hours without putting them in danger, as long as I don't share body fluids with them. Ha! Not much risk of that these days, as much as I wish I had a boyfriend to kiss.

I flip open my cellphone and call my eye doctor to see if I can reschedule my appointment that was supposed to be this Friday, as it conflicts with a class. Hope she'll tell me I'm ready to return to wearing contact lenses. I feel dorky wearing my glasses today, but it's necessary because not only are my eyes irritated from the therapy, they're also radioactive and I don't want to make my contacts "hot."

Anyway, it's silly for me to fret about how I look, because it's not like this is the sort of place where I could expect to earn an "MRS degree." Although male students outnumber female students by about ten to one, nearly all the men are preparing for the priesthood.

The emphasis on vocation makes the experience of being here far more intense than I had expected. When I arrived at nine-thirty this morning for orientation, I thought the talks were just going to be about rules and regulations. I wasn't expecting that the school's president, Fr. Boguslawski, would draw from St. Thomas on wisdom, knowledge, and understanding, and how the pursuit of these things draws us into a closer union with the Trinity.

Father's words transported me back to my conversion experience, when I heard that mysterious feminine voice saying, "Some things are not meant to be known. Some things are meant to be understood." And before I knew it, I was taking off my glasses and digging in my purse for something to soak up my radioactive tears. That was when my last tissue got used up.

Unfortunately there was no wastebasket within throwing distance, so I had to put the tissues back in my purse until the talks were over. Now I am trying not to think about the possibility that my entire purse is contaminated.

Thirteen minutes later. I feel awe entering the gorgeous Gothic-style chapel lined with stained-glass windows and painted inscriptions in Latin.

At first I take a folding chair along with some other laypersons in the back. It's not clear to me whether non-Dominicans are allowed to sit in the regular pews, which are set up in the old-fashioned style, facing each other across a central aisle. I don't want to draw attention to myself by marching up where I don't belong. But when I see that other lay students are in the pews, I move up so I can have a seat with a kneeler. Having that extra bit of comfort matters, as I'm still feeling a bit faint.

The wooden pew seats have hinges so that they can be flipped up. I pull one down so I can sit; it falls with a loud *plunk*! So much for trying to be inconspicuous. I might as well have brought a whoopee cushion.

Fifteen minutes later. I was not expecting that everything would affect me so much.

Fr. Boguslawski is preaching about today's reading from the first letter of St. Paul to the Thessalonians. I listen to him repeat Paul's words about how the Gospel "did not come to you in word alone but also in power and in the Holy Spirit and with much conviction" and once more am taken back to the words in the night that changed my heart.

Since my pew is perpendicular to the sanctuary, the most natural place for my eyes to fall is not upon the altar but upon the central aisle. And directly in front of me in that aisle is a stunning gold-toned statue of an expectant Mary. How appropriate, since I have felt lately that the Lord wants me to draw closer to her. All this year, as I went through my thyroid-cancer odyssey, I sought out writings that would help me understand who she was and who she wanted to be for me: Joseph Ratzinger's *Daughter Zion*, Maximilian Kolbe's reflection "Who Are You, Immaculate Conception," Pius X's Marian encyclical, René Laurentin's *Short Treatise on the Blessed Virgin Mary*, the Marian section of Eugene Boylan's *This Tremendous Lover* . . .

The words I heard that night in 1999 about knowledge and understanding replay themselves in my mind. For the first time I consider how Marian they were and how Thomist was their wisdom. Mary didn't just know God. She *understood* him, receiving him in her heart as well as her womb. And through the understanding that the Lord placed in her sinless heart, she was brought into union with the Holy Spirit and so entered into the Trinity's own exchange of love as much as is possible for a human person.

Just last night I told a friend over the phone that those readings had helped me understand that I had been afraid of the woman St. Maximilian called the *Immaculata*. I was afraid of her purity. But now I am beginning to understand that her purity is not something that is closed to herself alone. Although she alone is immaculate, she reaches out her hands, as she does in the image on the Miraculous Medal, because she wants us to share in the graces that have been given to her. Her "yes" is God's gift to us, to me. I want to share in it. She wants me to.

My mind turns to all the things I have wanted for my career these past several years that I have not received. I remember two years ago when I was told I was the top candidate for a full-time position at National Review Online—only to have my hopes dashed when the website turned around and hired someone else. Other disappointments come to mind. And I realize that the Immaculata has always been calling me to her. The message has been the same throughout, but I didn't realize.

I have not felt this way since that experience at the *New York Post* when I knew St. Maximilian had to be praying for me. Where I am, right at this moment, is where God wants me to be.

I want to have this feeling always.

More radioactive tears. Time to take out the napkin I grabbed in the lounge.

The greeting of peace already? Now that I've been crying and wiping my nose and mouth, I can't give anyone a handshake. So I keep my hands together, clutching the radioactive napkin, and try to make up for my seeming rudeness with friendly smiles.

Seven and a half hours later. That was an expensive dinner, but it felt good to treat myself at the end of a long day. Now I really need to write about today if I am to remember it. The restaurant isn't crowded, so the wait staff shouldn't mind if I pull out my journal even though I am done eating.

I scribble quickly, trying to capture my thoughts before they fly away:

"It is good for me that I was afflicted."

It occurs to me that perhaps I was allowed to suffer

this so that so many people would pray for me, bec I have been resisting and also suffering ignorance of my vocation for so long—this has been such an obstacle to my happiness—part of the source of the "existential angst" I was diagnosed w/long ago & never quite managed to shake despite the dramatic healing of conversion. . . . I truly did need an influx of grace which God has allowed to reach me through the intercession of the Communion of Saints, in order to begin the next stage of the path He has set out for me.

Monday, January 12, 2009, 7:39 p.m. I was lucky to snag a seat in a booth not far from the stage. Pat Troy's pub is always packed on nights when they have Arlington Diocese Theology on Tap.

Tonight Fr. Peter Ryan, S.J., is speaking on bioethics. I'm eager to hear what he is going to say about the Vatican's new document *Dignitatis Personae*, as it seems to rule out a type of stem-cell research, *altered nuclear transfer*, that he's supported in the past. If he claims the document doesn't rule out such research, I will need to buck up my courage to challenge him, because I think it's wrong.

My cellphone is showing I have a message. There's just enough time to listen to it now before the lecture starts. I ask one of my seatmates to hold my spot and then dash out to find a place away from the sounds of loud conversations and the jukebox playing U2.

Just outside the front door is an old-fashioned phone booth. I come inside, hoping no one will need to use the phone, and shut the glass door. Then I flip open my cellphone and punch in the number for my voicemail.

The man's voice on the recording is faint. "Hello, Dawn? This is Fr. Canavan."

Fr. Francis Canavan! I know what he wants. The ninety-one-year-old Jesuit has been calling me nearly every day for the past week. If I hadn't given him a copy of my Theological Virtues paper when I visited him New Year's Day at the Fordham University Jesuit infirmary where he lives, he wouldn't be so worked up.

The main reason for my trip to New York City was to attend Midnight Mass at Notre Dame Parish on New Year's Eve. But since I was in town anyway, I wanted to visit Fr. Canavan and give him my paper because I knew he would be proud of me.

Fr. Canavan is the closest thing I have to a mentor. Really, he is my mentor. I became a fan of his through his book *Pins in the Liberal Balloon*. Discovering him was like discovering a modern-day Chesterton. Then my friend Mike Potemra at *National Review* helped me get in touch with him and, to my joy, Fr. Canavan became a fan of my writings as well.

But I may not have much longer to enjoy his friendship in this life. When we met on New Year's Day, it was clear that he was weaker than when I last saw him, and his short-term memory was declining.

I wanted him to read my Theological Virtues paper because it had an Ignatian theme and because I thought he would be proud I did so well on it. My topic concerned how St. Ignatius of Loyola's *Suscipe* prayer models the way in which the human person is to make a return of divine love. To my surprise, given how rigorous the academics are at Dominican House, my professor gave me an A-minus. I know grades aren't supposed to matter, but it was a phenomenal encouragement for me, given that I am only beginning to study theology.

Fr. Canavan did read my paper, and his response was more than I bargained for—the daily phone calls.

First he called to tell me how much he was touched by my insights into the *Suscipe*. He said that, even having prayed that prayer every day for nearly seventy years, he learned things from my paper that he had never known before.

Then he called to tell me that I couldn't end my studies with a master's degree. I had to get a doctorate so that I could teach theology at a Catholic college.

In the wake of Vatican II, Fr. Canavan explained, there had been a wave of dissent among theologians at Catholic universities. But now a number of small colleges were seeking to revive Catholic theological education. In the years to come, there would be a need for professors like myself to help such schools pass along the truths of the faith.

"Faithful Catholic colleges need faithful Catholic professors," he said.

I told my beloved Jesuit friend, as gently as I could, that there was no question of my getting a doctorate. My master's-level classes were difficult enough. I just didn't have whatever it took to do doctoral-level study.

But Fr. Canavan, in his humble way, would not take no for an answer. He next called offering to put me in touch with former students of his who could tell me what it was like to teach at Catholic colleges: "I called Bill Luckey at Christendom and he said you could call him. Here's his phone number . . ." A professional lobbyist could not have worked harder.

So I know well what he is going to say right now when I return his call, but I have to phone him regardless. He could die any day, and I don't want to have on my conscience that I failed to call him back.

"Hello?

"Hi, Father, it's Dawn calling you back. Sorry it's so noisy. I'm out and about, but I saw that you called."

"Have you thought about getting a doctorate?"

"Father," I sigh, trying to think of a new excuse. "To tell you the truth, I'm scared of teaching. It's like being a parent of thirty kids with no spouse."

"I was scared, too, when I started out," he replies.

And with that, he launches into a story about his first day on the job teaching at a high school when he was a young scholastic. A student gave him trouble. He had the student remain after class and asked him to explain what was wrong. The student responded by telling him frankly that he didn't know how to teach.

Fr. Canavan ends the story by telling me how much the student helped him by showing him the things that he was doing wrong. He learned from his own student and became a better teacher.

I can't take it anymore. This man is a saint.

"Father," I say, "I really don't think I'm cut out to be an academic. But if you really think I have what it takes, I'll try to push through to a doctorate."

"That's wonderful. All you have to do is try."

Thursday, July 2, 2009, 12:07 p.m. Every time I come to a daily Mass here in the Crypt Church of the National Shrine of the Basilica of the Immaculate Conception, I wonder why I don't do this every day.

Today I simply knew I had to be here. I have been too wound up since that brunch with Mom and Ron last Saturday.

When Mom emailed me a few weeks ago to say she and Ron were coming to Washington for a conference and would like to have brunch with me, I wanted to see them but wasn't yet ready to spend time with them one-on-one. So I asked if I could bring my friend Wendy, and Mom agreed.

I did the best I could to prepare Wendy for what Mom and Ron were like, why I had a falling out with them, and why it is so hard for me to be comfortable around them. And I thought she understood.

But afterward, when Wendy was driving me back to my place, all she would talk about was how nice my "parents" were.

I corrected her and said they weren't my parents but rather my mother and stepfather. I have a father and he is not Ron. But then Wendy just corrected her language and talked about how nice my mother and stepfather were.

Yes, I said, they are nice people. Everybody likes them. I'm not surprised she liked them. But didn't she see how my mother acted with me? How she only asked me once, during our entire lunch, how my life was going? And then, when I tried to answer, she quickly changed the subject back to herself. So she's not really interested in me as a person. She thinks she is, but she isn't.

But Wendy wouldn't listen. She said maybe my mother was just nervous seeing me for the first time in months, and I should be more patient with her.

She doesn't understand. No one understands. Everyone thinks I'm being a mean daughter. As if this separation wasn't hurting me as well as Mom.

So I am here to visit with Jesus on a weekday, because I can't wait until Sunday. Maybe he will understand. And to be with Mary. Maybe she will understand too.

Half an hour later. The organist is playing the preparation hymn, but I don't feel like singing. I would rather watch the priest prepare the altar.

My gaze turns to the bracelet on my right wrist. Sr. Marla Marie gave it to me; its wooden beads are lacquered with

photographs of icons of Maronite saints. The one I am looking at right now is an image of Mary called Our Lady of
Lebanon.

Mary. She is everywhere here at the basilica; it's "Mary's
House." Just walking from the front entrance to the Crypt
Church, I passed by dozens of Marian shrines and statues.

Why is it so hard for me to get close to her? I know the
theology about her mediation. I pray for her intercession
every day. But why is it so hard for me to really *feel* that she
loves me?

That is a question I need to work through—not only for
the sake of my relationship with my mother but also for
myself. Teaching is a form of spiritual motherhood. If I am
ever to be a good teacher, I need to know how a mother is
supposed to love.

*Dear Mary, please show me how a mother is supposed to love.
Please let me feel your love.*

I think about my own mother. How she must miss her
own mother, my dear Grandma Jessie. Her separation is
worse than mine. She can't hear her mother's voice on the
phone like I can.

*And Mary, please be a mother to my mother. Please visit her and
let her feel your love too.*

Ten minutes later. Just received Communion. Back
in my pew and kneeling now as those in the pews behind
me go up to receive.

Have I ever received the kind of mother-love that I would
imagine Mary would have for me?

Yes. I have. Sr. Gerry loved me that way.

The memory of Sr. Gerry takes me by surprise. Tears. I
reach into my purse and fumble for a tissue.

An idea comes to me. I will pray.

Dear Mary, you know I want to feel your love. But I don't know how. So I am going to imagine that Sr. Gerry is standing in front of me, to the side of the altar. And I am going to imagine her opening her arms to give me a hug, and I will, in my mind, walk up to meet her. And what I would like is for her to stand in for you, so that when she hugs me, it is really you hugging me through her. Then I can begin to feel the motherly love that I know you want to give me.

I do this, stretching my imaginative powers as far as they will go. And I do see Sr. Gerry as she appears in my memory.

Her smile is just as joyful as I recall, and her eyes are just as bright, only no longer blind. And she does hug me. And I imagine that her love is Mary's and that Mary's love is hers.

At this moment, I sense that, in a real way, God has loved me through every human being who has ever loved me. And that where his love is, there is Mary's love too. And that, during Sr. Gerry's lifetime, Mary truly did love me through her. And that now, as Sr. Gerry is united with God in heaven, so too her love and Mary's love for me are fused.

They reach me together—the love of the motherly friend whose face I can picture with my mind's eye and the love of the Mother whose face I can see only with the eyes of my heart.

At this moment, Mary begins to be real to me.

About the Author

Dawn Eden Goldstein, whose previous books include *The Thrill of the Chaste* and *My Peace I Give You*, began her writing career as a rock and roll historian, using the pen name Dawn Eden. In the 1990s, she contributed to *Billboard*, the *Village Voice*, *Mojo*, and *Salon* and co-wrote *The Encyclopedia of Singles*. She went on to work in editorial positions at the *New York Post* and the *Daily News*. At the age of thirty-one, Goldstein, who was raised Jewish, experienced an encounter with the divine, which began a personal transformation that would eventually lead her to enter the Catholic Church. In 2016, she became the first woman to earn a doctorate in sacred theology from the University of St. Mary of the Lake. She is an assistant professor of dogmatic theology in the online division of Holy Apostles College and Seminary and lives in Washington, D.C.